The Traveler's Touch

The Footsteps of a Good Person are Ordered by the Lord

Jarrod D. Dixon

DEDICATION

I dedicate this book to my "Good Thing," Cynthia.
Just look at what our Awesome God has done with your victory dance!

ACKNOWLEDGMENTS

I would like to honor all the persons in my life whose encouragement made it possible for me go from thug to drug-dealer to preacher to mentor to Certified Christian Counselor to Nationally Published Poet to Author, for such a time as this.

My heavenly Father God and my Lord and Savior Jesus Christ.

My beautiful and anointed wife Cynthia.

My two sons and my daughters-in-law – Jiwann and Jarrod II, and Shadé and Seher.

My parents – Mr. and Mrs. Artemas Dixon

My brother and his family – Keir, Sherry, and Noah.

My Pastor, Rev. Dennis W. Bishop.

My dear deceased grandmothers, Evelyn Pearson and Georgia Dixon.

My dear deceased father-in-law, Sandy Witherspoon.

My father and mother-in-law, Mr. and Mrs. Rev. William Payne, Sr.

My First Waughtown Baptist Church family.

My brothers and sisters-in-law.

My good friend and fellow writer, Mr. Bobby Templeton.

My Vintage Bible College family.

My Hanes Brand Incorporated family.

And last but certainly not least, all of my relatives and close friends!

Without all of you, there would be none of me. God bless you, and I love you.

"Great minds discuss ideas; average minds discuss events; small minds discuss people."
- Eleanor Roosevelt [1]

Thus, this book is for great minds!

CONTENTS

INTRODUCTION

Dorothy had the company and companionship of the Scarecrow, the Tin Man, and the cowardly Lion to comfort and sometimes coach her on her quest to return back home to her farmhouse in Kansas. As this team of odd misfits travelled an unknown course set with perilous obstacles, along their journey to the Emerald City to seek the Great and Powerful Wizard of Oz, Dorothy was forever transformed with the new knowledge of priceless life lessons.

But in this story, you, also known as "So-and-So" (for the sake of anonymity), are unexpectedly visited by an extraordinary ethnically diverse family of nine colorful, charismatic characters to enlighten and empower you, literally, on your unexpected journey, set with life-changing vicissitudes of life. As you travel an unknown course to a place of self-discovery, in which your method of transportation is an "emotional rollercoaster" with no GPS, except for the inspiring directions of a team of mysterious Travelers each possessing the supernatural power of a "heavenly touch," you too, like Dorothy, are bound to be the blessed beneficiary of precious lessons on life.

So, if you are a lifetime fan of the Wonderful Wizard of Oz like I am, then you will enjoy this inspirational tale – *The Traveler's Touch, Part 1* – and perhaps even spread the word.

Grab your smoothie. Strap on your virtual reality goggles. Fasten your seatbelt. Experience this awesome adventure vicariously through "So-and-So." And enjoy! Afterwards, go and change the world. Show us what you can do with…well, you will just have to wait and see.

Nevertheless, congratulations in advance.

"The steps of a good man are ordered by the LORD: and he delighteth in his way."
- Psalms 37:23, KJV

BETTER THAN GOOD NEWS

"For as he thinketh in his heart, so is he…"

PROVERBS 23:7, KJV

A storm is coming. A mad storm.

It has been detected on radar by weather satellites. Its location is off Venezuela's coast in the Southern Caribbean. The storm descends from the star-spangled heavens like a gargantuan, galactic entity, and steps onto the water's floor between the Caribbean Sea and the North Atlantic Ocean. The waves rage and the winds roar with each footstep. This potent storm is so potentially violent that even the moon, high above Earth's atmosphere, is cautious and concerned. Nearly two-hundred and forty miles upwards from human inhabited land—beyond the troposphere, stratosphere, mesosphere, thermosphere, at home in the exosphere—the moon, with his eyes deadlocked onto this diabolical storm, takes cover and peeks out from over the shade of his blanket of black fog.

The moon's retreat proved to be a wise move. This tropical storm has now been upgraded to a hurricane by NOAA, the National Oceanic and Atmospheric Administration. This monster of a storm is already at Category 5 strength! Some might call this the "Finger of God," and others might call it an "Act of God." All I know is that we, the human inhabitants of this land way beneath the moon, are in dire need of God's Divine protection from

9

this mad storm!

The Caribbean Island nearest this abominable creation of nature is immediately warned of its coming. Consequently, the Carnival celebration, the biggest and most important event on this island's cultural and tourism calendar—a celebration that is electric with calypso and soca music in the air, explosive with a Masquerade Costume Band parade, organized stick-fighting tournaments, and limbo competitions, and erupting with wining dancing at block parties on every street—is rudely interrupted by the nation's government. *"The party is over! Scram! NOW!!"* The relaxing, enjoyable tropical island breeze is no longer relaxing and enjoyable. Thus, the Carnival celebration is officially cancelled mid-activity for obvious reasons.

This monstrous storm is a monstrosity in comparison to its predecessors that wreaked havoc on a smaller scale in comparison to the level of violence upon civilization committed by this guilty, galactic, gargantuan ghoul!

A great being came down from the sky unannounced and planted his feet on the Caribbean Sea, then began walking north of the Atlantic Ocean until his footsteps led him on a journey that no other storm in history with the magnitude of a Category 5 hurricane has ever traveled! And as he gets closer and closer to his target, his footsteps gradually mellow out.

This mysterious and mystical gentleman of extraordinary poise, of amazing savoir faire—with a heartbeat that sounds like a non-stop romantic instrumental balled with distinct emphasis from the harp, flute, and xylophone sections of an opera symphony orchestra—casually strolls along lonesome hallways, around sudden corners, and into the shadows of cold corridors.

With effortless swagger, calm as the calm after an angry storm, he descends gloomy stairwells. He ascends radiant staircases. His purpose leads him across exquisite balconies and dangerous breezeways, and even onto tranquil rooftops.

The dignified vampire-like stranger is coordinating from

head to toe in all charcoal, wearing a Fedora hat with lavender feather, buttoned-up trench coat, scarf, and suede gloves, and a purple cane as his sole accessory. Finally, the debonair traveler, who is cool as late November in Harlem, reaches his destination. And he doesn't look too happy. As a matter of fact, his villainous facial expression displays extreme hostility. In other words, this presumed nefarious "walking nightmare" looks as mad as the devil!

He has hypnotic onyx marbles instead of human eyeballs, and stands seven feet tall. His noticeably erect posture reveals he has somehow successfully eluded Father Time. He is broad and brawny—three hundred pounds of chiseled granite muscle—and chillingly charming, despite his long, silky, silver dreadlocks which reveal his longevity. "Intimidating individual" is an understatement for this mountain of a man, whose mannerisms sort-of resemble the actor Ving Rhames.

As a former "bad guy" myself, who is thankfully redeemed and delivered by my Lord and Savior Jesus Christ, I recognize the disposition. If this jolly gentleman is actually a hired assassin from the Virgin Islands, woe be unto the "job assignment" who is on his hit list. My friend, that is an angry storm I would not want to get caught in! You would be much safer trapped inside a farmhouse while caught in a mean twister in Kansas.

Is he a man? Or is he an angel with no wings? Or could he be a demon with no home address? His bass-heavy baritone voice is paralyzing. His accent is of the Caribbean Islands. His disposition is of Another World.

Finally, the angry storm reaches its destination!

And here comes the rain.

We all experience terrible "storms" in life. What can we do to prevent the storms of life from ringing our doorbell? Nothing. What can we do to prevent the storms of life from huffing and puffing and blowing our front door down? Nothing. What can we do to stop the storms of life from raging, from roaring, and from ripping up everything that we have worked so hard to build and obtain? Not a thing!

It behooves us to learn to dance during our rainy seasons. But, "Life isn't about waiting for the storm to pass…It's about learning to dance in the rain." [1]

Understand that it pays to study the storms of life and learn to recognize their modus operandi. If there is one thing I have learned during my forty-eight years on this "third rock from the sun," it is that everyone and everything has a methodology; has a method of operation. I have learned that different storms are designed to expose different weaknesses and exalt different strengths. And I have also learned that different storms are designed to explain different enigmas.

Every storm, by nature, has a distinguished methodology. For example, a tropical storm's degree of damage can sometimes be chaotic. A tornado's degree of destruction can potentially be catastrophic. And a hurricane's degree of devastation is often cataclysmic. Therefore, it pays for you to earn a PhD in "the method of operation of the storms of life." What is preventing you from earning your "degree in Meteorology"?

If you have ever experienced any degree of a storm in your life, then God expects you not to become a "master" over your storms, but a "Meteorologist!" If you have experienced the storm of doubt in your life, then *today* you ought to have your PhD in Meteorology. If you have experienced the storm of depression in your life, then *today* you ought to have your PhD in meteorology. If you have experienced the storm of disappointment in your life, then *today* God expects you to earn your PhD in meteorology! Again, I propose and present to you this thought: What is stopping you, hindering you, preventing you from learning to dance during your rainy seasons?

Life isn't about waiting for the storms of life to pass…it is about learning to dance in the midst of your storm! Selah.

The once happy, clear, and sunny sky is now charcoal

gray and looks wicked—very wicked. "Nebulous" is an understatement for this nightmarish noonday stirred up by naughty Mother Nature.

Tall, deep-rooted trees are uprooted one-by-one by an unseen and unnatural evil claw. This invisible foe lifts heavy-duty trucks, minivans, SUVs, and sedans into the air with ease and then drops the vehicles one-by-one upside-down onto the asphalt. As this invisible menace marches up the street, roofs of attractive split-level homes are peeled off one-by-one like an overworked Band Aid. Golf-ball-size hail bombards already destroyed automobiles and damaged houses. Live powerlines unloosen and fall to the soaked cement, as telephone poles snap like breadsticks.

You are home alone tucked into your dry bathtub, still wearing your favorite old, raggedy, torn Pittsburgh Steelers pajamas. You're on your knees in the proper elementary school safety position, trembling in terror and praying fervently and effectually. Suddenly, all of your windows are shattered, then sucked out. Guess where you are now? Unfortunately, yes. In the eye of an angry F4 Tornado! With insane wind-speeds of two-hundred and sixty miles per hour! Two hundred and sixty reasons for you to call on the Name of Jesus more intensely!

As your aching body is balled-up in your bathtub, terrified by this treacherous trial of tribulation, you continue to pray even more relentlessly, even though this psychotic cyclone is relentlessly attempting to murder your psyche. The combination of this deadly spinning funnel cloud in which you are helplessly imprisoned, along with the now ghostly quietness, is enough to drive anybody storming mad!

One-by-one, the minutes slowly pass. This invisible supervillain, who seems to have a personal grudge against you, stands over you and stares down at you like a vengeful cyclops. One-by-one, your fiery prayers begin to fizzle. One-by-one, your steadfast faith begins to flee. You're choked-up, coughed-up, tangled-up, twisted-up words begin to silence, until…

"Hello, and good morning. Are you So-and-So?"

The big fella is a rather scary dude. I mean, the cat looks like the Death Angel on steroids! So, you are an incy wincy bit terrified.

"Yeah…I   mean…yes,   sir.   That's   me,   sir."

"Splendid. I have something I would like to give you."

"Oh? Oh, really? What is it? I hope it's some…some good   news."

"Ha, Ha, Ha. Now, So-and-So, why would I want to bring you some bad news? Do I look like a messenger of bad news to you?"

Check out my unintimidated, unmitigated disposition toward "bad news."

"Tribulation, back again?
Absolutely unwanted.
Absolutely unwelcomed.
Absolutely uninvited.
A fugitive with many felonies;
all Home Invasions.
The expression on my face;
the polar opposite of delighted.

You're a messenger of bad news.
You psychologically violate whomever you choose.
You celebrate as your victims cry the blues.
You brag and boast about how you never, never lose.

With you, there's no compromising.
No negotiating.
No deliberating.
With you, there's no compassion.
No reevaluating.

No hesitating.

You're an immortal who cannot be tamed.
You're the master at your game.
Everyone knows your name.
Every generation is knowledgeable of your fame.
But TODAY history will be made.
TODAY is the day you taste the agony of defeat.
Bad news? Welcome to my arena.
Against me, from hereafter, get used to getting utterly BEAT!
Because GREATER is He that is in me, than ALL of the bad news that is in the world!"

Now you are trembling, and stuttering even more.
"No. No, sir. Not at all, sir. You…you look like you're a…like you're a really swell guy, sir."
"Ha, Ha, Ha, Ha! Believe it or not, I get that a lot, everywhere I travel. But getting back to business, what I am going to give you is indeed more exceptional than mere good news, So-and-So."
Like a man-eating tiger, he shows off his scary choppers as a scare tactic to paralyze his prey. His upper and lower canine teeth are pure gold, twenty-four karats, and look like daggers. He removes one glove. He reaches out his huge hand, dazzling diamond-studded gold rings on each finger, and gently places his palm in the middle of his job assignment's belly, then rubs in a circular motion with quick strokes, as if he were smearing on something magical. Or extracting something detrimental.
He looks like he can easily afford a fleet of showroom-floor charcoal Cadillac Escalades with custom lavender leather interiors, but this mysterious gentleman, for some odd reason, chooses his alligator-skin Stacy Adams as his sole source of transportation. This mysterious gentleman is called…*Imagination*. You are probably thinking that that's a weird name for a hit man. But then, if you think about it,

most hired assassins in those bloody, violent movies have cool, sometimes weird nicknames.

A few seconds later, your eyes open. You awake from your slumber. It's morning. Thirty minutes ago there was an angry storm that was thundering and hailing and raining felines and canines! But today the sun is shining magnificently.

You sit up. You yawn. You stretch out your arms. It is a new day. You are a new person...with new ideas...lots and lots of splendid new ideas! You pause and think aloud to yourself, "Yep. This is *Better Than Good News*."

Good news is not guaranteed. Good news is not always predictable. You don't have any control over the ultimate outcome...that's just the facts of life. However, "Imagination" can ignite faith that will enable you to handle the outcome, if it is not "good news!"

Before you hasten to your laptop and Google "Golden Lightning Bolt Ministries," "VisionFuel Marketing Consultant Firm," or "CleverGenius.com," go and change the world. Show us what you can do with your stroke of genius, your creativity, your marvelous imagination. I just showed you mine.

Congratulations in advance!

Hold up! Listen. Hear that? Sounds like footsteps. Ahhhh yeah. Imagination's younger sister. Just wait until she lays her hand on you!

SOMETHING WE ALL NEED

"Jesus said unto him, If thou canst believe, all things are possible to him that believeth."

-   St. Mark 9:23, KJV

There was an angry storm outside thirty minutes ago. But today the sun is shining magnificently! It's morning. You are now sitting on the edge of your king-size waterbed, fully awake, fully alive! There is an uncanny calm outdoors. Subsequently, you are overwhelmed with an undeniable gut-feeling that this particular day will by no means be just another mundane, run-of-the-mill, ho-hum, so-so, typical, ordinary day.

We are spirit and we possess a soul that lives in a body. Therefore, right at this very moment, during this exact instance, your spirit, your inner-self, is energized with the electricity of *imagination*; creativity, a "stroke of genius" from a Traveler's touch. As it turns out, he is not a demon. And for goodness' sake, he is not a vampire!

He is a friend who walked all the way from Trinidad, better known by her native inhabitants as "The Island of the Trinity," just to see you. Trinity, as in The Holy Trinity – God the Father, God the Son, and God the Holy Ghost. Whether you are spiritual or not or whether you are a Christian or not does not change the fact that the rich history of Trinidad was established on the Divine revelation that God Himself, along with His only begotten Son Jesus the Christ and the Holy Spirit, is The Most High of

Trinidad. Thus, today Trinidad is also known as "The Island of the Trinity."

Yes, you were touched on the belly by big brother Imagination, who traveled all the way from Trinidad. And so, the second journey begins.

You smile. You are smiling because you believe. You are smiling because you are hopeful and you are anticipating that something marvelous is going to happen to you today. You are smiling because deep within the depths of your soul, you believe that something miraculous, something "out of this world" is going to change your world, is going to change your life…today! Yes, Lord. Today, more than any of the previous days of your earthly existence thus far, you are seeing, you are visualizing, you are conceptualizing, you are realizing, you are imagining that the proverbial glass of your life is not half empty. Oh no, on the contrary, it is half full. Yes, Lord! Half full.

Today you are smiling, because neither is your internal gas tank half empty. Neither is the reservoir of your mental perception, your mental capacity, your intelligence, your inspiration, your ingenuity, or your creative genius half empty. Neither is the reservoir of your determination, your willpower half empty, your will to fight, your resilience, your intrepidity, your fortitude, or your tenacity half empty. Neither is the reservoir of your hidden potential, your self-motivation, your self-esteem, or your self-confidence half empty. Today, you are smiling because not only is your internal gas tank half full, but today, even more than any of the previous days of your earthly existence thus far, your self-image is half full. Yes, Lord! Half full.

Here is what you must understand: having a "glass-half-full attitude" towards life is a very good attitude, mindset, and belief system to have. Question: What about your "belief system"? Is the proverbial glass of your life half empty today? Is there anything, any type of energy, any type of force, any type of superpower deep within the depths of your soul for you to rely on to help you persevere through the storms of life for the remainder of your earthly existence?

You hear footsteps. However, these are not the footsteps that belong to a mortal human being. These footsteps are light as a lavender feather, yet heavy as a charcoal Cadillac Escalade. They are quiet, like the first falling snowflake softly landing upon the pavement of an unusually unoccupied Chicago street. At the same time, they are as loud as a roar of thunder followed by Mother Nature's fireworks display of golden lightning bolts!

A pair of feet land softly upon a street like a set of twin snowflakes fallen from a cloudless, completely gray mid-winter sky. The street is vacant. In fact, all of the streets are vacant! However, all of the stoplights appear to be functioning normally.

As the footsteps boldly approach the first stoplight, it suddenly changes from red to green. This may sound a little looney, but *all* of the metropolis' stoplights change immediately from red to green the second she steps toward them. The instant her feet touched the pavement, this entire metropolitan city became a ghost town. Imagine that!

This mystery woman puts one foot in front of the other with purpose, predetermination, and passion as she walks up naked avenues, down empty boulevards, and into desolate alleys. Now that I have your attention, I can discern the annoying questions that are reverberating inside your attentive brain:

"Who is this mystery woman?"
"Where does this mystery woman come from?
"What does this mystery woman look like?"

Well, let us deal with one question at a time, beginning with the latter.

Avigail Alfatov. Does the name ring a bell? I did not think so. But, I am sure you are going to Google it. Anyway, this mystery woman, this second Traveler of this second journey, is definitely not within the proximity of comparison of Lady Avigail Alfatov. In fact, Madame Avigail Alfatov should never even be mentioned in the same sentence as this mystery Traveler. No offense.

The royal princess-like stranger is angelic in her silver, ruby adorned tiara, alluring in her curve-clinging crushed velvet long-sleeved ruby evening gown with mid-thigh high split up left leg, majestic in her glittering silver open-toe high-heels, and authoritative in her black silk choker with an eye-catching authentic black pearl charm. This wondrous woman has long, straight, derriere-length hair – no weave – as black as the black pearl she wears around her neck. She has an hourglass figure like the mythical Greek Goddess Aphrodite, with the dreamy eyes, drop-dead gorgeous face, irresistible dimples, and billion-dollar "Colgate smile" of *all* of the Miss Universe Crown winners in the pageant's history. "Heavenly angel" is a shocking understatement for this wonder of a woman. Is she indeed a flesh-and-blood woman? An angel? Or something else? Whatever she is, she finally reaches her destination.

Her sensuous voice is packaged with compelling confidence. Her accent is of the nation of Israel. Her ambience is of Another World.

You are tucked into your dry bathtub on your knees in the proper elementary school safety position. You are still wearing your favorite choice of loungewear that you were wearing yesterday: white tank-top, a pair of baggy gray sweatpants, and thick, red, comfy thermal socks. You simply prayed yourself to sleep during that terrible storm. But how could you have slept for this long? Especially all balled-up in your bathtub? Who runs for cover and steps into their bathtub, gets into the tornado-warning safety position, and sleeps for twenty-four straight hours during a bad thunderstorm that only lasted about thirty minutes?

Perhaps there really wasn't an angry storm outside at all yesterday? Perhaps you didn't actually run for cover and step into your bathtub at all yesterday? Perhaps the reason you are still wearing the same things you had on this same time yesterday is because in reality yesterday is today? Maybe all of this is one big crazy dream. But maybe…it's not!

Was Imagination just a figment of your wild imagination? Or was he real? And if he was real, how was he able to travel by foot all the way from Trinidad to your house? I bet he has some seriously ugly blistered corns on the side of his pinky toes! And some serious callous bunions on his big toes! Seriously. From all of that walking? Just think about it. It doesn't make sense. But then again, the fact that you survived an F4 tornado with insane wind-speeds of two-hundred and sixty miles per hour doesn't quite make sense either! But I guess the most puzzling part of this mystery is, how did you end up in your bed? The last thing that you remember is the effect the combination of the deadly spinning funnel and the ghostly quietness had on your rationale. To put it more plainly, the last thing you recall is the twister tap-dancing on your brain to the point where you almost lost your sanity.

However, it is a good thing that today you still have your sanity. Yes, today you are in your right mind. Today you have a sound mind, a strong mind, a stable mind. But how did you end up in your bed? Unless…

"Hello, and good morning. I presume you are So-and-So?"

"You presume correctly. I'm So-and-So."

"Wonderful. I have something that you need."

"Is that so? Well? If it's something that important, then I guess it won't hurt to try it. Right?"

She smiles and giggles.

Do you know the difference between a want and a need? Believe it or not, some people get the terminologies twisted. It is, though, a logical oxymoron. It has always been quite easy to confuse the two, because there are times when a need can feel like a want, and a want can feel like a need.

Case in point: Adam and Eve assumed that they *needed*

21

that forbidden piece of fruit for their nourishment. But, in actuality, they both really *wanted* to "become as gods."

Case in point: King David assumed that he *needed* to bathe in Bathsheba's love. But, in actuality, he really *wanted* to bathe in his own lust for Bathsheba.

Case in point: The Prophet Jeremiah assumed that he *wanted* to shut down his prophetic/preaching ministry, his "Kingdom assignment," or rather, his divine job assignment. But, in actuality, he really *needed* the peace-of-mind from being obedient to his calling to "preach the Word of God in season, and out of season." Why? Because The Word of God was like a fire shut up in his bones! Where are all of my fellow anointed preachers at?

Thus, I have come to the conclusion that I *want* wealth and riches but, in actuality, I *need* Jesus! I *want* fame and fortune but, in actuality, I *need* Jesus! Throughout the decades—and I thank God that today I can say—I have discovered the difference between a "want" and a "need." Therefore, I have come to the conclusion that I *want* a few million in the bank. But, in actuality, what I really *need*…is Jesus! Where are all of my fellow Christians at?

Well? Is it a want or a need? Is it a need or a want? What we all need to do is quit calling a want a need, and just keep it one hundred, and call a spade a spade! If it looks like a duck, if it waddles like a duck, and if it quacks like a duck, then…

"Well, So-and-So, this is something that you will need to rely on for the remainder of your earthly existence."

Then she reaches out her beautiful hand and tenderly wipes the right cheek of her job assignment's bewitched face. Now, to address your first question with an answer, the name of this mystery woman, who chooses her footsteps as her "navigated vehicle," is…*Faith*. Yes. Faith…*Something We All Need*.

As you sit on the edge of your bed "cheesing," it dawns on you that you have just experienced a wonderful life-changing epiphany! Now, it is time for you to hop up off of that waterbed, go to school or go to work and work your faith, because faith without works is dead. If you can imagine it, then you can achieve it. But you *must* rely on faith…your faith!

It makes perfect sense to me as to why the first Traveler, big brother Imagination, would journey all the way from Trinidad, also known as "The Island of the Trinity."

"And the LORD said, Behold, the people is one, and they have all one language; and this they begin to do: and now nothing will be restrained from them, which they have IMAGINED to do. Go to, let us [The Holy Trinity] go down, and there confound their language, that they may not understand one another's speech" (Genesis 6-7, KJV).

In this familiar story of the tower of Babel, it was the unified people's power of imagination that drove them to build this remarkable tower. Our first Traveler, Imagination, can relate extremely well to the "power of imagination." It was the incredible potential of imagination that actually got the attention of the Holy Trinity!

Thus, it is also logical to me as to why Imagination's younger sister Faith would travel all the way from Israel, where Father Abraham, "the father of faith," traveled throughout touching lives.

As I conclude, I exhort you to go out and change the world. Show us what you can do with your power of belief. And all of us will be waiting with great anticipation and immense excitement, for the grand arrival of your "it."

Once again, my friend, congratulations in advance.

This is beginning to be a lot of fun. Fasten your seatbelt, because I hear more footsteps. So far, you have been impregnated with Imagination and Faith. Awesome! But get ready! Here comes Faith's younger sister.

And if you thought the touch of Faith was powerful, you are about to spring to your feet!

SPECIAL DELIVERY

"In Gibeon the LORD appeared to Solomon in a dream by night:

and God said, Ask what I shall give thee."

- I Kings 3:5, KJV

The country of Tanzania, in East Africa, is the famous home of Mount Kilimanjaro. Mount Kilimanjaro, the fourth tallest mountain on planet Earth and the tallest mountain on the continent of Africa, is the tallest freestanding mountain in the world. And what I mean by "freestanding," is that here on its territory of Tanzania – the most famous safari on planet Earth, Mount Kilimanjaro stands alone! However, this monumental mountain is not *really* alone.

Near the foot of Mount Kilimanjaro resides a pride of lovely but lethal East African lions. Mama lion is out shopping for fresh antelope for her hungry family's dinner later this afternoon. Her five male cubs are simply adorable! They are having themselves a heaven of a time; playing, wrestling, and chasing each other.

Bid daddy, also known as "king of the jungle," is close by keeping a protective eye on his scrappy, rambunctious youngin's. All of a sudden, out of the corner of his watchful right eye, he barely catches the tail-end of something moving…*fast!*

Surprisingly, our next Traveler does not walk. She runs!

And she runs FAST!!!

Isn't it amazing how God sometimes allows a specific prayer request to be miraculously manifested in our lives...*fast*? Whoever invented the popular phrase "I didn't see that coming" should be awarded some type of prestigious award in his or her honor. Personally, I regard this phrase as "the Super Bowl's Vince Lombardi Trophy" of personal victory! When God blindsides you with a blessing that you have recently requested of Him in prayer, and *fast*, it simply amazes you! When God blindsides you with a miracle, *fast*, it simply astonishes you! When God blindsides you with that answer, *fast*, it simply baffles you! When God blindsides you with divine revelation knowledge, *fast*, it simply bedazzles you! When God blindsides you with that "open door," *fast*, it simply blows you away! When God blindsides you with that "golden opportunity," *fast*, it just simply blows your mind! And that's simply the kind of God I serve—a mind-blowing God!

Now please don't get me wrong. I am not so heavenly-minded, that I am no earthly good. I am at all times consciously aware of the potentiality of "Murphy's Law." Meaning, I am fundamentally in-touch with reality. Yet, I also possess a "measure of faith" that tells me, "Nothing is impossible with my God! Absolutely nothing!" I understand that sometimes it takes days to receive our breakthrough. I understand that sometimes it takes weeks to receive our peace. I understand that sometimes it takes months to receive our change. And I understand that sometimes it may even take years to receive our victory. Yet, I also know that sometimes God will move on your behalf...*fast!* For the Bible tells me,

"God is our refuge and strength, a very present help in trouble.

Therefore will not we fear, though the Earth be removed, and though the mountains be carried away into the midst of the sea;

Though the waters thereof roar and be troubled, though the mountains shake with the swelling thereof. Selah" (Psalm 46:1-3, KJV).

Sometimes the pressures of life can swell-up on you and attempt to overtake you. Therefore, sometimes God becomes "your very present help in trouble," and *fast*. And sometimes the perplexities of life can swell-up on you and attempt to overpower you. Therefore, sometimes God becomes "your very present help in trouble," and *fast*. Sometimes God will bless you with a blessing so mind-blowingly *fast*, that the only thing you can say is, "Thank you Jesus! I didn't see that coming!"

The footsteps of a good person are ordered by the Lord. And if you are reading this book right now, the Lord has led your footsteps, via divine providence, to read these words right here: In the Lord's eyes, you are special! Isn't it amazing how the world can be so cruel, and treat you so cold? Unless you were born with a silver spoon in your mouth, you may be able to relate with the ideology that this world is a cold, cold world!

When you are up, the world is your pedestal. But when you are down-and-out, the world is your undertaker! Isn't it amazing how fast the world tries to give you the standing eight count, even while you are brawling with your adversity? Isn't it amazing how fast the world tries to rule you out of the race, even while you are running the marathon? And isn't it amazing how quick the world tries to lay you in the casket, speak two or three good words about you at your funeral, then toss the dirt onto you in your grave, even while you are fighting the good fight of faith?

Man, this world is a trip! This world will trip you and cause you to stumble and fall flat on your face! Then, in a heartbeat, this cold, cold world will write your obituary. If you don't believe me, then you better ask somebody! This world will trip you and cause you to stumble and fall flat on your face! Then, in a New York minute, this cold, cold world will have the audacity to say, "Stick a fork in him, because he's done!" If you don't believe me, then you better ask somebody! This world is a trip! This world will trip you and cause you to stumble and fall flat on your face! Then, in a Jumpin' Jack Flash, this cold, cold world will spit on your grave! And if you don't believe me, then you better ask your next door neighbor!

Like I said, our next Traveler does not walk. She runs! And she runs *fast*!

So picture this, and try to keep up…if you can. She is running neck-and-neck with a herd of stampeding rhinoceroses. Then, she shifts into another gear, and leaves them in her dust.

Next, she catches up with a herd of racing zebras. She pulls up to them. Then she pulls ahead of them. And then she disappears out of their sight.

Next, she catches up with a playful herd of leaping gazelles. This time, instead of foolin' around and teasing them, she decides to simply blow right past them like the wind!

At last, she meets more challenging competition. She catches up to a gliding cheetah, sprinting at his top speed of seventy-five miles per hour! Running neck-and-neck, the poor dumbfounded cheetah stares at her in total disbelief. She notices from her peripheral. She looks at her competitor. She smiles, winks her eye, and blows him a friendly kiss. Then, she zooms ahead, vacuuming all of his spots off his well-conditioned frame; not literally, of course.

Her bare feet, a blur to the human eye, hit the surface of the Atlantic. You already know what happens next. Bingo! Just like the comic book superhero The Flash, she jets across the ocean as if it is an Olympic track! This heartbreaker is such a handful that 9-time Olympic gold medalist Usain Bolt, even at the top of his game on his best day, cannot handle. She sprints onward to North America.

Using your imagination, picture this: A seventeen year-old Pocahontas. She has a lot more pep in her step than the Walt Disney Movie Pocahontas. You know what I mean? Well, let me just put it this way: While the Walt Disney movie Pocahontas scampers, the "Pocahontas" in this chapter scats! There's a big difference.

Only four feet, eight inches tall, she is genetically blessed with a well-conditioned physique that recalls the late three-time Olympic gold medalist Flo Jo to memory. Her shiny hair is the color of 1:00 a.m., cut short and worn in a cute, sassy bob. And howbeit, her bare feet are clean, dry, and flawless! This spectacular, spunky speedster, with her glossy scarlet toenails and lipstick, reaches her destination.

Her voice is as promiscuous as her personality. Her accent is Native American Indian, of the Ancient Pueblo Indian Tribe, to be specific. Vivacious and flirtatious, this PYT ("Pretty Young Thing") is something special! And her quintessence is of Another World.

What good is it to have an abundance of imagination, but no faith to bring these splendid ideas to life? What is the ability of creative genius worth if you lack the faith to birth it out of you? As a matter of fact, why would big brother Imagination even bother to travel three-thousand miles, by foot if his younger sister Faith would not have been able to show up after him? It would have been a huge waste of his time, because without Faith, imagination is just a nice, luxurious brand new Cadillac Escalade with custom lavender leather interior, but without any wheels. Now that sucks!

If Imagination is the vehicle, then his sister Faith has to be the wheels! This is the thought that you reason with and rationalize as you sit on the edge of your bed with one fist on your upper-thigh and your opposite elbow on your other thigh, while you are holding up your chin with your finger and thumb, looking like The Thinker sculpture in Paris, France.

Your house is still spinning and swirling in the eye of the tornado, but you don't seem to notice anymore. As the storm tosses your house about, your full attention is elsewhere. But? Are you dreaming? Or are you awake? These are good questions to ponder. Meanwhile, you glance down at your comfy red socks and wiggle your toes. You begin to lighten-up. You loosen-up, and then you grin. You think silently to yourself, *I bet ole big brother Imagination could use a pair of these right about now, after he finishes soaking those poor old barking dogs in a tin tub with hot water and Epsom salt. Three-thousand miles by foot. Yeah, right.* Then you chuckle.

Once again, your mind drifts back to try to remember when you got up out of your bathtub and climbed up in your bed and crashed-out. Finally, your memory is starting to cooperate. The answer is being processed and is beginning to compute. This great mystery is about to be solved, until…

"Hello, and good morning. Glad I caught up with you before you stepped into the shower, So-and-So."

"Hey? Where did you come from? And how do you know my name?"

"You'd be surprised how much I know about you. I could be your guardian angel."

She smiles and winks her eye. She continues.

"I have something for you."

"Special delivery?"

"Honestly? Everything I deliver is special."

Then, she springs into the air from off her pretty little tiptoes. She levitates. Yes, she does that too. And then she gives her job assignment, you, a sweet sisterly kiss on your left cheek.

Suddenly, while you have yet to budge from your spot on the bed, you are jolted by a sizzling, tingling sensation, and you spring to your feet! And in a blink of an eye, your uninvited intruder is a "ghost."

Interesting. Is she a ghost? That is a good question. Or could she actually be your guardian angel? Well, consider her big brother's touch, and use your imagination. I will share this bit of insight with you: this light-footed, lead-foot, likeable, petite Pocahontas sweetheart's name is…*Gifted.* And do not let her youthful aura and anatomy fool ya. Baby girl's tribe dates back seven-thousand years, give or take a couple of days.

Now, let us turn the corner.

29

Like I said in the onset, in the Lord's eyes, you are special! If you have any doubts today that you are special in the eyes of the Lord, then get this:

You are so special that the Lord has ordered your footsteps and has allowed you, via divine providence, the chance to get your hands on a copy of this book, so that He can speak to you through these prophetic pages. You are so special that the Lord has ordered your footsteps and has allowed you, via divine providence, to be able to dodge the fiery darts of the Enemy, so that you could be in the right place at the right time, so that you could get your hands on a copy of this book, so that the Lord can speak to you through these prophetic pages.

The footsteps of a good person are ordered by the Lord. So make sure you keep your feet clean! Because a pair of nasty, cruddy, stinking ole feet is not a pretty sight in the eyes of the Lord!

So, while you are standing on your bare feet, do a few jumping jacks or a few push-ups to get the blood flowing, because you have just been gifted with something special! Now go and change the world. Show us what you can do with your special gift that was given to you via *"Special Delivery."* Go ahead. Reveal that phenomenal gift to the world, as I proceed to reveal mine to you.

Congratulations in advance!

You have been touched by Imagination, who traveled all the way from Trinidad; "The Island of the Trinity." Therefore, today, you are blessed with an awesome imagination, which is *Better Than Good News*.

You have been touched by Faith, who traveled all the way from "The City of David" – Jerusalem, the capital of Israel. Therefore, today, you are blessed with strong faith, which is *Something We All Need*.

And, you were touched by Gifted. Although she resides in North America and is a Native of the Ancient Pueblo Indian Tribe, she traveled all the way from the continent of Africa, through the safari and across the Atlantic Ocean.

Therefore, today, you are blessed with a phenomenal gift via *Special Delivery*.

Now, wasn't that thrilling rollercoaster ride exhilarating? Hold up! Hear that? What? More footsteps? Indeed.

Let's see. Now that you are gifted, you cannot escape from wondering who the fourth mysterious Traveler will be. I will give you a hint. He is Gifted's older brother. And just like an older brother would do, he is always coming behind his baby sis and wiping up her spills. Unlike her, "foolin' around" is not in his vocabulary.

THE GIANT'S GIANT

"A GOOD name is rather to be chosen than great riches,

and loving favour rather than silver and gold."

-    Proverbs 22:1, KJV

A seasoned male golden eagle soars majestically with a demeanor of governing dominion. Surveying his kingdom, thus protecting his domain, this kingly father symbolically covers his family, which is partaking in suppertime within the comfort and safety of their nest upon the zenith of a Himalayan Mountain fifty feet below, with his remarkable wingspan. From an altitude which is near humanly unsustainable, being that it is the world's highest region, the regal bird circles the sky, then heads downward.

Now, let us follow the Yellow Brick Road.
Hanging rock, after hanging rock, after hanging rock.
Hazardous ridge, after hazardous ridge, after hazardous ridge.

A man descends the tallest of the Himalayan Mountains as if he had been accustomed to doing it since he was a toddler. Apparently, he and this mountain are acquainted, just as he is with the family of golden eagles who are now six-thousand feet above him. He and this mountain, known as Mount Everest, are close friends—they seem like they're childhood chums, even! This strange fellow is physically capable of mastering such a frightening feat with such finesse, because he himself is "one with the mountain!"

He looks as if he could be a Tibetan monk of twenty centuries ago, as he is draped in a goldish gown down to his mocha cowhide sandals, and wrapped in a handwoven crimson robe. Black beads and red beads swing from around his neck and sway at his navel-area. Nearly thirty-thousand feet later, from the summit of the tallest mountain on planet earth, he finally reaches his destination.

He has a mediocre physicality and unimpressive appearance. He stands only five feet, four inches tall, and the scale reads only one hundred and forty-nine pounds. At first sight, this below-average, adult-male, great-grandfather, with his elderly shaven cranium, is just an irrelevant old-timer. But before we judge a book by its cover, is he actually "below average"? Is he actually "irrelevant"? Though seemingly elderly, possibly a great-grandfather, and visibly a plain old-timer, is he actually human?

His voice is meek and mild. His accent is East Asian. His preeminence is of Another World.

On another note, take a moment to ponder this thought:

"With great power comes great responsibility." [1]
– Uncle Ben in the Spider-Man Movie

Your gift will make room for you and bring you before great men. And I am pretty sure that if you hang out with baby sis Gifted long enough, she will personally escort you to and introduce you to all kinds of great men. Your gift will eventually take you to the top. Again, if you were to hang out with Gifted long enough, she would get a kick out of pushing you, pulling you, chasing you, dragging you, fussing at you, encouraging you, and coaching you all the way to the top of your game. You see, she may be young (maybe not chronologically), but Gifted is smart enough to know that if a person stays at the top of their game long enough, then the sky's the limit!

When your gift has finally reached its destination, you will find yourself standing on top of the world! You can order anything on the menu, because the sky's the limit baby! Ahhhh yeah. When your gift has taken you all the way up to the zenith of Mount Everest, you can order *anything* on the "menu of life," because the sky's the limit! If you are a single woman, and if you have an appetite for the man of your dreams, if you are standing on top of the world, then this specific gentleman is on your menu sister, because the sky's the limit baby! If you are an eligible bachelor, and if you are ready to settle down with the woman of your dreams, if you are standing on top of the world, then that special gal is on your menu brother, because the sky's the limit!

Ahhhh yeah. Your gift will make room for you and bring you before great men. Your gift will have you dancing and singing on the apex of Mount Everest. Your gift will take you to the top, and have you standing on the top of the world. If you stay at the top of your game long enough, your gift will eventually reach its destination. And then you will be able to order anything on the menu, because the sky's the limit baby!

Who would want to come back down from living in the clouds on the highest mountaintop in the world, when they have lived all of their life at the bottom? Who would want to come back down after finally having a taste of the "good life," when they have lived all their life at the bottom? Who would want to come back down from standing on top of the world and ordering anything on the menu that their heart, their mind, or their body craves, when they have lived all their life at the bottom? I cannot think of anyone who actually loves living their life at the bottom! Can you?

In the Gospel according to Saint John, chapter ten, verse ten, Jesus said, "I am come that they might have life, and that they might have it more abundantly." Amen? Now, when Christ said "they," our Lord and Savior is referring to you and me. And when the Son of God mentions that they might have "it" more abundantly, the Prince of Peace is referring to a stress-free life. And in my opinion, a stress-free life is the good life!

So then, how can you constantly maintain a peace-of-mind when you are living life at the bottom, all your life? How can you constantly maintain a stress-free life when you are living life at the bottom, all your life? How can you constantly maintain a happy spirit when you are living life at the bottom, all your life? I mean, is it truly possible for anyone to actually love living their life at the bottom, all their life?

Your gift will make room for you and bring you before great men. Ahhhh yeah. Baby sis Gifted would definitely have herself a blast escorting you all the way up to the pinnacle of Mount Everest…where the sky's the limit baby! But I must warn you, if you were to ever lose focus, get a big head, or forget where God has brought you from, there is a very high probability of you finding yourself slipping over the edge of your "mountaintop," unless…

"Hello, and good morning, So-and-So. I pray you are healthy, sane, and prosperous."

"Well? Two out of three. I'm healthy, and I'm somewhat prosperous."

The strange stranger grins and nods.

"That will do. I have something that will help you magnanimously."

"Magnanimously? Sounds hard to refuse."

"I would not have spoken it if it were not so."

Then he reaches out his thin, short arm, and drops his wrinkled hand on the ball of his job assignment's right shoulder.

Within the eternity of that same second, you glance at your right shoulder, realizing the reality of the touch. However, there is no evidence. His identity? I am delighted you asked. This fourth Traveler, this giant of a gentleman who humbly chooses to hike everywhere in his mocha cowhide sandals, goes by the name of…*Character*.

Do you know the definition of "fun"? Fun is "someone or something that is amusing or enjoyable: an enjoyable experience or person." [2] Only three letters long. Fun. A word that is often used by seven and eight-year-old little boys. Fun. A small word that almost instantly puts a smile on your face, as soon as the "n" leaves your lips. Even the very thought of this cute little word brightens-up your eyes. Fun. A word that is hardly ever used by high school teenagers. Fun. A word that is almost never used by homeless people. A cute little word that has cost many their marriage, their family, their health, their financial security, their home, their reputation, and even worse…their life!

But how can a cute little word like "fun" be so…costly? If having fun was a crime, then we humans might as well all become robots! If having fun is a sin, then we humans might as well all become Pharisees, or Sadducees, or nuns, or monks. How can a cute little word like "fun" be so…dangerous? You see, fun helps you to forget all about your worries, problems, troubles, and heartaches. Fun helps you forget about your struggles, failures, and mistakes. Fun helps you forget all about your enemies. Fun helps you forget all about all the negativity in your life today! So, how can a cute little word like "fun" be so costly and dangerous?

If fun were to be totally subtracted from your life, then how often or how seldom would people see you smile or laugh? If fun was completely missing in your life today, just how happy do you think you would be with your life? If fun is so scary, why did God create joy? If fun is so naughty, why did God create laughter? If fun is so mischievous, why did God create us humans with the ability to smile? How can a cute little word like "fun" be so…bad? If having a little fun every now and then is such a bad thing, why isn't it illegal? Why does it relieve so much stress? If having a little fun every now and then is such a bad thing, why are there circuses, amusement parks, zoos, aquariums, movie theatres, state fairs, carnivals, ski resorts, and Broadway plays?

If having a little fun every now and then is such a bad thing, why are there comedy clubs, nightclubs, book clubs, bowling alleys, roller skating rinks, public parks, and golf courses? If having a little fun every now and then is such a bad thing, why are Disney World and Disney Land such great escapes from a world that is filled with reality?

Could it be that fun requires balance? Could it be that fun requires moderation? Could it be that fun requires maturity? Or could it be that fun requires plain ole common sense?

If something is such an enjoyable experience that you have traded in your wholesome lifestyle for it, then maybe it is time for you to start using your plain ole common sense…before it is too late. If someone or something is so pleasurable that you no longer have a good reputation or a moral compass, then maybe it is time for you to consider using your plain ole common sense, if you still have any left…before it is too late!

Fun. How can a cute little word like "fun" not be so…fun?

The measure of a man's integrity is not what he gets from his ancestors, but what he leaves his descendants.

If I may, let me say this: a REAL MAN leaves behind *"an inheritance to his children's children: and the wealth of the sinner is laid up for the just"* (Proverbs 13:22, KJV).

In other words, what God is saying in His Word to us menfolk is that a fake man does not consider blessing his children in some way or another because he is too busy thinking about himself. Nor does the fake man consider leaving behind a blessing, or blessings, to his children in some form or fashion. Because the fake man is too busy thinking about himself! Do you know any fake men?

A real man, however, is always thinking of creative ways of blessing his children. A real man, however, is always thinking of what blessings he can leave behind to his children…and to his children's children! Do you know any real men?

Exercising integrity takes practice. And practice makes perfect. The more I exercise integrity, the closer I get to becoming a true disciple of my Lord and Savior Jesus Christ. Because, you see, it is very easy for me to hold my head up and stick my chest out and broadcast to everybody that I am a disciple of Jesus Christ. But when the rubber meets the road and I am forced to decide whether I am going to man-up or not, the Spirit is indeed willing, but the flesh is weak, and so my integrity is often put to the test.

Speaking of tests, I remember quite a few years ago I used to despise these "integrity pop quizzes." They used to really get on my nerves! I used to feel as though God was just picking on me for fun and laughs, knowing all along that I was not thoroughly prepared for the test. I have a college degree in Christian counseling, and one of the many things I have learned as a student of higher learning is that your score on your test will expose the truth of whether or not you took the time and made the sacrifice to thoroughly study your class material.

I no longer hate integrity pop quizzes. This is because I have since then discovered an invaluable secret. Whenever your integrity is tested, God is setting you up for greatness! Whenever your integrity is tested, God is setting you up for promotion! Whenever your integrity is tested, God is setting you up for increase! Whenever your integrity is tested, God is setting you up for advancement! Whenever your integrity is tested, God is setting you up for elevation! Whenever you are hit unexpectedly with an integrity pop quiz, God is not picking on you for fun and laughs. Whenever you pass these tests of your integrity, God is actually setting you up for a raise. A heavenly handsome raise!

In the Old Testament, when Brother Jabez prayed, he was daring enough to ask the Lord God Jehovah of Israel to expand his territory. Well, I have likewise prayed the

"Prayer of Jabez." Why? Simple. It is my heart's desire for the Lord God Jehovah of the Christian Church – the God of the Old Testament and the God of the New Testament – to expand *my* territory, so that I will be able to leave behind an inheritance to my children's children…like a real man!

"He (Jabez) was the one who prayed to the God of Israel, "Oh, that You would bless me and EXPAND MY TERRITORY! Please be with me IN ALL THAT I DO, and keep me from all trouble and pain! And God granted him his request" (I Chronicles 4:10, NLT).

So today I am conscious about the measure of my integrity. And though I might have failed many pop quizzes and retaken them until I passed them in order for me to arrive at this place in my life, today my lifestyle reveals that I am a real man who is setting my children up for greatness, setting my children up for promotion, setting my children up for increase, setting my children up for advancement, setting my children up for elevation…because the apple doesn't fall far from the tree!

The measure of a man's integrity is not what he gets from his ancestors, but what he leaves his descendants.

So let us exercise integrity *in all that we do.*

Still frozen in your spot, you lay your left hand on your right shoulder, and pat it twice. Then you head to the kitchen to get a cold bottle of water.

Your world has just been twisted inside-out and flipped upside down! Your natural thought process has just been re-invented! Your mind has just been elevated by an old, puny Tibetan monk, who appears as if he could barely bench-press a hiking stick! Nevertheless, his level of integrity qualifies him to be honored among giants, as a "giant among giants!"

Now go and change the world. Show us what you can do with your inspiring integrity, with your captivating character! As for myself, God is not finished with me yet.

Congratulations in advance!

Let's see. So far, big brother Imagination. Big sister

Faith. Baby sis Gifted. And yesterday, you received a visitation from a fourth Traveler named Character, *"The Giants Giant"* – a little old man with enormous integrity! The only thing he's missing is a halo.

So by now, you should already know what to expect. My "element of surprise" has ran its course. Now the question is not "will there be another uninvited guest?" but *how* and *when* will he or she show up?" But this time…no spoiler alerts. No hints.

Sorry.

THE PRINCIPAL THING

"Trust in the LORD with all thine heart; and lean not unto thine own understanding.

In all thy ways acknowledge Him, and He shall direct thy paths.

Be not wise in thy own eyes: fear the LORD, and depart from evil."

- Proverbs 3:5-7, KJV

"So-and-So? So-and-So? Wake up, So-and-So."

You awake, though only partially conscious. You wipe the slobber off the corner of your bottom lip. Then you look down at the puddle of saliva that you have been snoozing in for the last hour and a half.

"Finally."

You glance up at the voice.

"I have been calling your name for five minutes…because class ended five minutes ago."

The voice belongs to your philosophy professor.

"I just came very close to calling the university paramedic. Wild party last night?"

You return back to Earth.

"Wild party? Who are you? And where am I? I was just standing in front of my refrigerator, gulping down a bottle of water…wasn't I?"

Your instructor responds with a touch of sarcasm.

"If that is what you choose to imagine. By the way, that is quite an imagination you have."

The tough professor smirks with arms folded. With a pair of outdated, unfashionable reading spectacles balancing across the protruding bone of her nose, the strict, sharp-dressed senior citizen philosophy professor sort of resembles iconic actress Mademoiselle Helen Mirren. And by-the-way, her excellency is of Another World.

The time is 7:00 a.m. on the dot. Noisy, hectic streets are packed with near bumper-to-bumper traffic. Seems as though everybody is busy and in a rush to get somewhere on time. Police sirens, ambulance sirens, firetruck sirens, and a variety of automobile horns all blend together to compose the soundtrack for this big city's early morning downtown scenery.

A taxi's rear passenger door slams shut. The passenger steps out, carrying a burgundy leather briefcase. Acres upon acres of golf course-green courtyard is almost as lively as downtown itself! Male and female students socialize, while the majority scurry inside to their morning classes. A professor, who is in no rush, casually strolls across the courtyard, dividing the crowd of young adults, en route to the entrance of the building. A sign reads: Istanbul University.

Knowledge is power!

However, this is an understatement. Knowledge is so powerful that God warned us in His Holy Scriptures that without it His people are destroyed! *Destroyed!* Wow! They were destroyed for lack of knowledge. Now that's deep. And if God did not intend for us, His people, to take heed of His admonition, then He would not have spoken it.

I understand that not every graduating high school senior will have the opportunity to go to college. This is a sad reality. But because we are living in a time of national economic crisis, this is a reality nonetheless. This is why I thank and praise God for every single college scholarship fund organization throughout the United States of America whose main goal is to try and help as many aspiring and qualified high school grads achieve their dream of being accepted and enrolled into an accredited institution of higher learning.

Higher learning is power!

However, this too is an understatement. Understand that higher learning is so powerful that, although he walked with, talked with, lived with, worked ministry with, suffered with, bled with, cried with, laughed with, celebrated victory with, and broke daily bread with The Master for three solid years during Christ's earthly ministry, John—the beloved disciple who was banished to the Isle of Patmos to live the rest of his life in exile and die alone—was encouraged by God to come up higher!

"Then as I looked, I saw a door standing open in heaven, and the same Voice I had heard before spoke to me like a trumpet blast. The Voice said, 'COME UP HERE, and I will show you what must happen AFTER THIS'" (Revelation 4:1, NLT).

If you have a "measure of faith" to believe this, then you should not have a problem with receiving what I am about to impart.

If you are reading these words, wherever you are, whatever state of mind you are in, whatever condition your lifestyle is in, God – through me– is exhorting you to COME UP! COME UP HERE! COME UP HIGHER! Do you know why colleges and universities are often referred to by scholars as "Institutions of Higher Learning"? Affirmative! Knowledge takes you HIGHER! You see, everyone has an "after this." Understand that your "after this" is located right between your "today" and your "tomorrow." So then, today God is encouraging you to come up higher, then after this your tomorrow is going to be brilliant!

Today! Come up higher! Then after this, your tomorrow is going to be breathtaking!

Today! Come up higher! Then after this, your tomorrow

43

is going to be beautiful!

Today! Come up higher! Then after this, your tomorrow is going to be exceptional!

Today! Come up higher! Then after this, your tomorrow is going to be exciting!

Today! Come up higher! Then after this, your tomorrow is going to be extraordinary!

I exhort you in the name of Jesus Christ of Nazareth, to COME UP HIGHER today. Then after this, your tomorrow will be the location where God needs you to be, for such a time as this.

Understanding is power!

However, this is also an understatement. Understand that understanding is so powerful, that God basically said in His Holy Scriptures, if you don't obtain anything else in life, if you don't glean anything else from life, if you don't grasp anything else out of life, please, please, please, please grab hold tight of understanding and do not let go!

"…with ALL thy getting GET UNDERSTANDING" (Proverbs 4:7, KJV).

After you finish reading this chapter, I hope that you will grab hold of understanding, and that you won't let go! After you finish reading this book in its entirety, I hope that you will grab hold of understanding, and that you won't let go! After you go to sleep tonight, then wake up in the morning, I hope with immense hope that you will get all that you can get from understanding, and that you will hold on tight and won't let go!

Ya know, they say that experience is the best teacher. Well? I think it is time we set the record straight, end this nonsense, and tell "they" that they are dead wrong! Throughout the course of this forty-eight-year-long journey, which I am still traveling, I have had a plethora of teachers, some good, some bad. But trust me, experience has never been my best teacher! But I will give experience a lot of credit. Experience has taught me a lot of lessons in life, some light, some hard. However, experience has by no means been my best teacher.

You know, they say experience teaches you the difference between right and wrong. I don't know about you, but I disagree. Experience, rather, teaches us how to choose what we think is the right thing or the wrong thing. And experience may teach us how to go in or not to go in the direction that we think is the right way or the wrong way. Due to the fact that sin is running so rampant in our world today, not even experience, with all of its expertise, can help everybody see clearly and judge correctly whether something is right or wrong. Because the truth of the matter is, today we are living in a time when "they" are calling wrong right, and calling right wrong. Amen? Clearly, even they are confused themselves!

If experience is the best teacher, then why is it that we sin so willingly and so frequently when the Holy Bible tells us clearly that "the wages of sin is death"? If experience is the best teacher, then why are there ex-convicts among our societies today who become repeat offenders, habitual offenders, and career criminals, even after being taught hard lessons from experience by being incarcerated for most of their lives?

And to further add validity to my conviction, if experience is the best teacher, then why is it that spouses continue to be secretly unfaithful to one another, even though the same immorality of infidelity devastatingly costs them their previous marriage? If experience is the best teacher, then why is it that managers and executives continue to get caught embezzling from their employers, even though they had been charged guilty for similar illegal activities in the past? If experience is the best teacher, then why is it that so many of our U.S. Government officials and politicians continue to get caught-up in so-called concealed extra-marital affairs that sabotage their careers and destroy their family legacies, even though they have traveled down this road several times before and discovered that it often leads to a dead end?

You know, they also say that you can't teach an old dog new tricks. Well? I don't know about that. But what I do know is that experience is vital. However, experience has its limitations. I admit, I have some notable experience in a number of different arenas in life, priceless experiences that have earned me a certain level of success. Still, if I could revisit my past and redo some things, no, redo a lot of things, then I would have sought the Lord for a teacher who was far more experienced than experience –a Divine Teacher!

I am elated to say that for the past twenty-six years of my life I have had a personal relationship with such a Divine Teacher. And His name is the Holy Spirit! I have found out that the Holy Spirit provides for me and equips me with an inner "Counselor" – a "Wonderful Counselor" – who clearly and truly shows me the difference between right and wrong. So you see, you can have all of the experience in the world, but until…

"So-and-So? Now that you have joined us back here on the third rock from the sun, I have something that I need to give you."

"Okay. Whatever it is, I hope it will help me wake up from this weird dream."

She chuckles, then smirks.

"My dear, I assure you that after today you will never again be awakened to this degree."

Guess what today is? Today is the day of your New Beginning. Today is the first day of your wonderful, wonderful, wonderful Spiritual Transformation! My friend, I decree and declare that today is the day of your Spiritual Awakening! What is so awesome about today, what is so astounding about today, and what is so "awakening" about today is that regardless of whether you are already currently active in your ministry, your calling, your Kingdom assignment, guess what? Today is the day that even you are only seconds away from experiencing a supernatural, divine, heavenly, miraculous metamorphosis!

If you do not believe a word I am saying, then I guess you can stop reading right now, and close this book. That is on you. It is your future. If you do not believe a word I am imparting, then that is on you. It is your future. And if you do not believe a word I am prophesying, then, my friend, that is on you, because it is your destiny. But if you believe, then prepare yourself...

"Jesus said unto him, 'IF thou canst BELIEVE, ALL THINGS are possible to him that BELIEVETH'" (St. Mark 9:23, KJV).

...for LIFTOFF!!!

Let's get lifted.

1. Today is the day that you will experience the feeling that something has changed inside of you!

You cannot find the words to describe it, but today you feel different. You even experience the sensation of being mysteriously transformed into a new person. Today you have a new attitude, a new outlook, a new perspective, a new mindset. The world now has a new appearance. The world now has a new color, simply because you are now viewing the world, including your world, with a pair of new eyes! Today is the day of your Spiritual Awakening.

2. Today is the day that you will experience an unusually uneasy awareness of your old bad habits.

You are becoming aware of everything that is not right in your life. This, my friend, is no ordinary sense of awareness. This kind of awareness is shifting you to a place of the new you. Thus, you realize that as of today, you no longer desire to do all of the things you used to do that were illogical, immoral, unethical, and ungodly. This is due to the shift in your thinking pattern, the elevation of your thought process, and the enlargement of your thought capacity. Thus, today you feel deep fulfillment and happiness. You are getting closer and closer and closer to the "truth" of who you really are! Today is the day of your Spiritual Awakening.

3. Today is the day that you will experience the feeling

47

of the need to make this world a better place.

You, for reasons beyond your reach, are increasingly growing dissatisfied with the notion of *only* taking care of you and *only* taking care of your four, and no more. So today enough…is not enough. You have an insatiable urge to want to make a difference in the lives of others. You have an insatiable thirst to want to help others become successful and victorious. You have an insatiable craving to want to have a positive impact on the lives of others. You are experiencing an overwhelming, overpowering, and uncontrollable hunger to want to holistically change others' lives…forever! As of today, you have fundamentally ceased from being a selfish individual. So today, taking care of you and your home, your house, your family, your four *only*, is no longer enough! Today is the day of your Spiritual Awakening.

4. Today is the day that you will experience a deep yearning for meaning in your life.

A lot of sights you used to see, pleasures you used to partake in, places you used to go, and things that you used to do are not as fantabulous, not as fulfilling, and surprisingly, not as "fun" to you anymore. This is simply because now, right now, you need meaning in your life. Sights and pleasures and places and things that ordinary people find to be a most fun-filled, euphoric experience, is now simply boring to you. Period. You are now realizing more and more that small minds are blown away by people and pleasure, average minds are blown away by places and material possessions, but *great minds* are stimulated by self-discovery! Today is the day of your Spiritual Awakening.

5. Today is the day that you will experience the sensation of hypersensitivity.

In addition to your five physical senses– sight, hearing, taste, touch, and smell – which are becoming more and more developed and heightened, even as you are reading these words, your spiritual senses – intuition, emotion, imagination, conscience, and inspiration – are also increasing at a phenomenally high speed! From this day forward, your intuition will show you things you have never seen before, your emotions will reveal things you have never seen before, your imagination will open your mind, open your eyes to things you have never seen before, and your conscience will be enlightened by things you have never seen before. And from this day forward, your divine source of Divine inspiration will lead you, will guide you, will direct you, will "order your footsteps" one step closer – day-after-day – to reaching your destiny in Christ Jesus, like you have never ever seen before! Today is the day of your Spiritual Awakening.

6. Today is the day that you will experience a level of enhanced creativity, a level of enhanced genius, and a level of enhanced inspiration which will all combine and work in unison to help you achieve all of your dreams!

Make sure your seatbelt is fastened tightly, because right at this moment, your life is in liftoff mode! Your mind, your being, your essence, your soul is about to be bombarded with wonderful ideas...all the time! You will receive unimaginable imaginations, unique ideas, and out-of-this-world lyrics and melodies for musical compositions. And you will receive a level of creativity, a level of genius, a level of inspiration which is sacredly reserved for the Heavenly host, for the angels in Heaven, for those immortal cosmic celestial beings who serve El Elohim – The Supreme, The Superior, The Sovereign Creator and Master of the Universe – all the time! Your level of creativity, genius, and inspiration will be in liftoff mode...*all the time!* You are getting ready to shed tears of joy! Because you are getting ready to reach out and touch your dreams. You are getting ready to live out your dreams. All of your dreams! All the time! Today is the day of your Spiritual Awakening.

7. Today is the day that you will experience increased personal phenomena. You will experience momentum in mysterious coincidences in your life!

You are growing spiritually at an incredibly rapid rate! And you love it! The more you grow spiritually, the more your positive energy grows. And the more your positive energy grows, the more you will understand how perfectly *everything* in your life is orchestrated, arranged, designed, and predestined by God…and by God alone! The people you meet will be the people who unknowingly help to birth out your greatness. The places your feet take you will be the right places where God wants you to be, and at the right time. The thoughts that you think will almost immediately become manifested, even while you are thinking them. Your presence will attract presents. In other words, your "is-ness" will become a magnet for money and magnificently marvelous movements and ministries. And your is-ness will become a magnet for miracles! Thus, you will helplessly wonder to yourself, *What in the world is going on with me?! What in the world is happening with my life?!* You will begin to see odd numbers out of the clear blue for "seemingly" absolutely no apparent reason at all. However, it will be these specific "odd numbers" that will change your life! And you will receive seemingly senseless revelation knowledge, which appears to make no sense whatsoever, from within your own spirit. However, it will be these specific spiritual revelations that will change your life! Your is-ness is about to introduce you to your greatness! And yes! You love it! Today is the day of your Spiritual Awakening.

8.   Today is the day you will experience a Christ-like willingness to love freely and to give cheerfully, without reward or repayment.

After you finish reading this particular chapter, and once you have fully accepted and fully received the prolific prophetic potency of these pages, then you are going to look around and feel like a total "misfit!" Why? Because you do not fit in or blend in with everybody else, nor do you feel comfortable thinking like everybody else! Therefore, you are now officially a misfit! You will be looked upon by your city, society, community, coworkers, close friends, family and relatives, and even some fellow Christians, as being a total misfit! Why? Because you have finally arrived at the destination of what it truly means to have Christian compassion, to walk in Christian love, and to "live to give, and give to live," as a child of God! Today everybody else expects something good in return for their sacrifice of love. Today everybody else expects something rewarding in return for their sacrifice of giving. But you, howbeit, are a total misfit! Why? Because you have discovered the secret of giving! You have realized that it is more blessed to give than to receive! So today it is my honor to share the title of total misfit with you, my friend and fellow Traveler. Be proud! Be grateful! Be peculiar! Be a MISFIT! Today is the day of your New Beginning! Today is the day of your Spiritual Awakening.

Your professor removes her unappealing bifocals and carefully adjusts them on your face. And then, she nonchalantly leans forward and puts her mouth close to your ear.

"WAKE UP!"

You jump! You drop your bottle of water, and it spills all over the kitchen floor. After you wipe the perspiration off your forehead and eyebrows, you shut your refrigerator door, stand still, and just begin to ponder. As you backtrack in your head, you reason with yourself aloud.

"Let me see now. First, I was rubbed on my stomach by Imagination. Next, I was wiped on my cheek by Faith. Then I was kissed on my other cheek by Gifted. Next, I was touched on my right shoulder by Character. So? What does this philosophy professor represent? She's as tough as an Egyptian taskmaster! And she is definitely no angel! Too old. Hmmm?" A few seconds later, you wisely solve the puzzle.

"I got it! Those hideous, ancient, senior citizen bifocals of hers! Wisdom!"

Ahhhh yeaaaah. Feels good, doesn't it? In Proverbs 4:7, the Bible says, *"Wisdom is the principle thing; therefore get wisdom:*

and with all thy getting get understanding."

Yes, yes, yes. *Wisdom* is the name on her birth certificate. By now, I know you are probably wondering to yourself, *Why would Professor Wisdom draw me all the way to Turkey? In my dreams?* Let me help you out with that.

Mesopotamia is the birthplace of civilization. Mesopotamia is between two historical rivers: The Tigris and The Euphrates. Well? The Tigris and The Euphrates rivers are the two rivers that surrounded The Garden of Eden. Thousands and thousands of years ago, the land known as Mesopotamia became the "Modern Day Garden of Eden." Today, Turkey, along with a few other countries on the continent of Africa, is referred to as modern-day Mesopotamia. And to tie this all together, if Adam had demonstrated wisdom in the Garden of Eden, then the world would not be in this mess that it is in today! Can I get an amen?

Feel free to use your own imagination. Or? Your own wisdom. Now go and change the world. Show us what you can do with your *"Principle Thing."* Show us what you can do with your divine insight. Show us what you can do with your King Solomon-like problem-solving ability. Lord knows the world could use more superheroes like you!

Congratulations in advance.

Here is where we hear those familiar sounds. Can you hear them? I certainly can. Loud and clear. Oh yeah! Closer and closer they get. And just when you thought you had finally crossed the finish line…surprise! More footsteps! Surprise! It's another Traveler! Traveler number six.

What an extraordinary family! Would you not agree? Diversity is a beautiful thing. Discrimination is the total opposite. And this fabulous family of Travelers is a heavenly work of art. Different races. Different nationalities. Different cultures. A diverse family of brothers and sisters united and blended to create a colorful masterpiece!

A big brother from a tropical island of the Caribbean Sea.

A big sister from the Middle East.

A little sister whose bloodline is of the oldest Native American Indian Tribe.

A big brother from the Himalayas.

A big sister from Turkey, by way of the ancient land of Mesopotamia, known as "Modern-day Garden of Eden," in which present day Mesopotamia consists of: Iraq, Iran, Kuwait, Syria, and Turkey.

And now, surprise! More footsteps, which belong to our sixth Traveler. March on, little brother. March on. We are eagerly awaiting.

UNLATCH AND UNLEASHE

"I can do all things through Christ which strengtheneth me."

-   Philippians 4:13, KJV

A brave lad unlatches a gate and lets a bull into a ring. The matador, standing firm and alone in the center of the ring, watches his young, fearless chief assistant wave his bright yellow and magenta cape in front of the bull to provoke him to charge.

A trumpet sounds, a team of picadores surround the bull, and hurl spears into the sides of this monster's muscular body, as if they are participating in target practice.

A second trumpet is blown and the suave matador removes his black, winged hat and dedicates the forthcoming death of the bull to the president of Spain. His ego is as big as the state of Texas. But in this particular circumstance, it is to his advantage. And he is as cool as the other side of the pillow in an artic Holiday Inn hotel room. This too should give him an edge.

Now, it is time for the faena. This is the part in the bullfight where the matador must prove his courage and artistry. In his left hand he holds a muleta, a short stick with a piece of thick crimson cloth draped over it. And in his right hand he holds the espada, the killing sword.

Now, it is showtime!

This show is basically a dance with death. One wrong

move and the suave matador could find himself leaking blood, lifted up and carried around the ring by the bull's horns, which are pierced clean through his ribcage, chest, and back. While trying not to become a human shish kabob, the matador must also amuse the audience with a dramatic, suspenseful, risky performance that will thoroughly entertain the crowd. Thus, his mission is to earn himself a thunderous standing ovation from them in the end. Two birds dead. One stone.

As the faena continues, the suave matador demonstrates his superiority over the raging bull. He dances and dodges. He dodges and dances. Standing ten feet away at all times, the matador has succeeded at making the bull dizzy and delirious. The crowd is anxious because now it is time to put one of nature's most intimidating killing machines out of his misery!

The matador attacks the bull with his espada, lodging his killing sword deep between the dazed bull's shoulder blades. Then, the matador snatches out the lodged weapon and begins to stab it into the severely wounded bull's neck until his spinal cord is severed. Almost immediately, the bull drops to his knees and collapses to his expected demise. The dance with death is over! The crowd goes crazy! Like I said; two birds, one stone.

The macho matador takes his bow before his honorable president first. Then, as he bows to his audience of hundreds of amped-up fans, they cheer and toss beautiful flowers down at his boots. His chief assistant then runs out into the ring and collects all of the flowers except for one, which he leaves for his boss. The suave matador bends down and picks up a single-stem red rose. When he rises, he is holding the thorny stem of the ravishing rose with his teeth and waving both hands high above his head as a show of victory. The electrified crowd applauds him and chants his name.

Spain's hero! He basks in his fame and glory! This celebrated matador is the man!

Now, it is time for Act II!

Some sports fans (I may indeed be the number one critic) are of the belief that baseball is not a contact sport. Therefore, it should not be compared to the NFL, the NBA, and the NHL. You must admit that today there are masses of people who are addicted to action! We are hooked on action films as if they're drugs! We are hooked on adventure and fantasy novels as if they're drugs! And today, lots and lots and lots of true sports fans, especially me, are hooked on contact sports as if they're drugs! I am hooked on heavyweight championship boxing! I am hooked on the NFL playoffs! I am hooked-on the NBA finals! I am a true fan of contact sports. Unless a professional athlete is knocking his opponent flat on his you-know-what, you will hear me snoring…loudly!

Los Angeles, California, "The City of Angels," is home to those legendary heavyweight champs the L. A. Lakers and the L. A. Kings. Because of all of the big movie stars and the shiny, bright, and often surreal nature of Hollywood and the movie industry, L. A. is also known as "Tinseltown." Because of the "Hollywoodish" state-of-mind that hovers thick in the atmosphere and the heavy focus on dreams, fantasies, frivolous endeavors, forbidden ambitions, hidden agendas, and a strong stigma that whispers "We are out of touch with reality" in the air, L. A. is also known as "La La Land."

The glitz, the glamor, and the glitter defines Los Angeles, which is known for red carpet events, the rich and famous, and the ravishing beauties. The golden sunshine, the paradise-like climate, the airborne go-getter epidemic, all combine to define the City of Angels. Speaking of angels, let's talk baseball.

Although it may not be one of my favorite subjects, the game of baseball is considered by many to be "America's Favorite Pastime." Iconic first ballot Hall of Famers such as the great number 42 Mr. Jackie Robinson, Willie Mays,

Hank Aaron, Willie Stargell, Reggie Jackson, Ken Griffey, Jr., and other greats all combine to define the history of the National League of Baseball. These game-changing gentlemen, these superior athletes who dominated the game of professional baseball, hit the hardest, ran the hardest, and threw the hardest! They set records. They broke records. And they won titles. Speaking of winning titles, let's talk Los Angeles Angels of Anaheim.

From 1979 to 2014, the Los Angeles Angels franchise has racked-up an impressive total of nine West Division titles. [1] This outstanding resume includes their 2002 World Series victory against the San Francisco Giants. A fantastic payday for L. A. Add this championship to the Los Angeles Lakers victory against the New Jersey Nets in the 2002 NBA Finals that same year, and it's another fantastic, fabulous payday for L. A. [2] Now let's do the math. In the year 2002, Los Angeles, the City of Angels, Tinseltown, La La Land, accomplished what other large cities across the U. S. dream about. In the same year, L. A. had TWO, not one, but TWO professional sports franchises that managed to reign victoriously in their respective arenas!

What a phenomenal, unfathomable, glorious payday for the City of L. A.! Sort of makes you want to make La La Land your next vacation destination, doesn't it? Talk about a city with prestige, with prosperity, and with paydays. Wow! I love L. A.! Speaking of payday, let's talk about C. J. Wilson and his $20 million-dollar arm.

C. J. Wilson is a pitcher for the Los Angeles Angels who signed an insane five-year $77,500,000 guaranteed contract in 2016, which included a ridiculous $2,500,000 signing bonus! [3] So as of 2016, C. J. Wilson's annual salary is a whopping $20 million dollars. I said $20 million! During his and his teammates' 2002 World Series win over The San Francisco Giants, C. J. Wilson's fastball averaged-out at speeds of ninety to ninety-three mph. [4] I said ninety to ninety-three mph! The velocity of a ninety mile-per-hour fastball equals one-hundred and thirty-two feet per second.

I said one-hundred and thirty-two feet per second! Let's do the math. A ninety mile-per-hour fastball that travels a distance of one-hundred and thirty-two feet per second, according to Sir Isaac Newton's second law of motion, is equivalent to eight-thousand, three-hundred and fourteen pounds of pressure. I said eight-thousand, three-hundred and fourteen pounds!

To give you a better picture of this pitcher's $20 million-dollar arm, getting struck in the temple of your cranium by a ninety mph fastball is about the same as standing and letting former professional heavyweight boxing champion of the world Iron Mike Tyson hit you with his best uppercut. I said Mike Tyson's best uppercut! To sum it all up, Mr. C. J. Wilson throws a hellacious fastball! Look the word up in your Webster's dictionary. And woe be unto the batter if a ninety mph fastball thrown by C. J. Wilson's $20 million-dollar arm hits him dead in the temple of his cranium! Speaking of getting struck in the head by "hellacious fastballs," let's talk about the mean fastballs of life.

Curveballs, unlike fastballs, are tricky and usually unexpected. However, a fastball is typically what all baseball players, from the little leaguers to the major leaguers, study, train, practice, and prepare for religiously. I said religiously! When you are struck in the head by "crafty curveballs of life," your initial verbal reaction is, "Oh BLEEP! Where did that come from? That BLEEP BLEEP curveball totally caught me off-guard!" Now a fastball is a horse of another color altogether. When your skull is cracked-open by "ferocious fastballs of life," due to the acceleration of the pitch, your initial response is, "JESUS!" I said Jesus! Speaking of Jesus, let's talk homeruns.

When you have Jesus in your life, and I am speaking from personal experience, you can take a bold swing at the mean fastballs of life, and whack a homerun! When you have Jesus in your life, you can take a bold swing at family issues pertaining to your children and your children's children, marital issues in your home, finance issues in your piggybank, and health issues in your body, and whack a homerun! When you have Jesus in your life, you can take a bold swing at immorality issues in your life, and whack a HOMERUN! Listen! Can you hear the "cloud of witnesses" up in heaven cheering for you? But seriously, I have a question for you. How good is your batting swing?

And now, the Final Scene – Act III!

Finally, the lad reaches his destination. Oh? So you assumed that the suave matador would be the sixth Traveler? Or his young fearless chief assistant? I apologize, but nope! After he unlatched the gate to let the bull out into the ring, the lad straightaway embarked upon his mission, trotting through the city of Madrid.

The brave lad, in his blue denim overalls, no shirt or socks on, a pair of raggedy unlaced dingy-white classic Chuck Taylor Converse sneakers on his feet and a backwards-turned all-red Los Angeles Angels baseball cap on his head, appears to be only a couple of years older than his younger sister. But he has a certain twinkle in his eyes to complement his "old soul" that suggests to all who meet him that this kid is not really a kid at all. Perhaps mainly because his demeanor is of Another World.

In the closing seconds of the eighth round of their highly hyped-up rematch, which was the World Boxing Council championship for the welterweight title belt, due to that unforgettable punishment Sugar Ray Leonard was putting on Roberto Duran, also known as "Hands of Stone," reigning champ Duran cowardly surrendered by crying to his opponent, "No mas, no mas!" [5] In English that means, "No more, no more! You're beating my doggone brains out man! Please stop hitting me! Ouch! You're hitting too hard man! I quit!" Nah. I added that last part for laughs.

I know you might be sniggling right now. But I know at least one person on this planet who was not laughing on Wednesday, November 26, 1980 at the Louisiana

Superdome in New Orleans, during prime time—Mr. Hands of Stone!

I love the quote by the late President Richard M. Nixon on the topic of never giving up.

"Defeat doesn't finish a man, quit does. A man is not finished when he's defeated. He's finished when he quits." [6]

Wow! Is that not profound? And propelling? Hey? Wait a minute? Propelling. I like that word. It makes me sound, well, profound. But on a serious note, what is it that propels you from within to never give up? What is it that propels you to keep going, when your circumstance is demanding that you throw in the towel, and cry out to your situation, "No mas!"? Or is your propeller broken?

Defeat does not flat-line a man, giving up the fight does!

Defeat does not end a man, throwing in the towel does!

Defeat does not silence a man, backing out does!

Defeat does not defeat a man, chickening-out does!

Defeat does not finish a man, quit does!

I make no apologies for preaching.

Once more I ask the question: what propels you to continue fighting the good fight of faith when the fight seems mighty unfair and fixed? Sometimes, fighting the good fight of faith appears to be futile. Sometime, fighting the good fight of faith feels like it's a ridiculous waste of time. Sometimes, fighting the good fight of faith feels flat out stupid. And sometimes, fighting the good fight of faith feels downright hopeless! But guess what? Sometimes—no, at all times—when we are drafted into a championship boxing match for the weight-class title belt, we must kick our feelings out of the driver's seat, grab hold of the steering wheel as tight as we can with both hands, and then put the pedal to the medal and yell out, "HERE I COME!"

Watch out trouble! Because HERE I COME!

Watch out problems! Because HERE I COME!

Watch out opposition! Because HERE I COME!

Watch out circumstance! Because HERE I COME!

Watch out situation! Because HERE I COME!

Watch out Sugar Ray Leonard! Because…uh…can I have your autograph? Yeah, yeah. Don't laugh! You would start singing a different song too if you came face-to-face with him in the ring. You see, unless…

The slim, slightly over six foot tall youngster reaches out his long, strong arm and extends his balled fist at your torso. He just stands there and stares at you like a zombie with his lips sealed, waiting. However, his non-verbal actions speak a crystal clear language which is elementary to you.

"Oh? Okay."

You bump his fist once with yours. The next thing you know, you're in front of your bathroom mirror, just standing there staring at your reflection with your lips sealed…like a zombie!

On that note, who is this mysterious Traveler? He is certainly not a zombie, like in all the Hollywood movies. And he is certainly not an Egyptian taskmaster like his older sister Wisdom. Even so, this brave lad is definitely an enigma. And that, my friend, is for certain.

It takes baseballs to stand and face the San Francisco Giants in your life.

Well? How can we overcome these *GIANTS?* That is a good question. Let's talk about it.

Me: "What's going on Jiwann?

Jiwann: "Hey Da."

Me: "What's up wit it, Lil'J?"

Jarrod, II: "What it do Dad?"

Me: "Y'all check this out. I have something I want to give both of you.

Jarrod, II: "For real?"

Jiwann: "Word?"

Me: "Word."

Jarrod, II: "I hope it's some money!"

Jiwann: "Yeah. Me too. Did you finally hit the Lottery?"

Jarrod, II: "You still playing the Lottery Dad?"

Me: "Hold up. Listen. What I have to give y'all is way better than money. Besides, the Bible says that the love of money is the root to all evil."

Jiwann: "The Bible said the love of money Dad. The love of money. So…"

Jarrod, II: "…But none of us loves money Dad. So…"

Jiwann: "…So, bless us with some money, Dad?"

Me: "Man! You two guys are something else. Look? This is what I have to give you."

"The Universal Zulu Nation stands to acknowledge wisdom, understanding, freedom, justice, and equality, peace, unity, love and having fun, work, OVERCOMING the negative through the positive, science, mathematics, faith, facts, and the wonders of God, whether we call Him Allah, Jehovah, Yahweh, or Jah." (Afrika Bambaataa) [7]

You can overcome that giant through Christ who strengtheneth you.

"The brave man is not he who does not feel afraid, but he who CONQUERS that fear." (Nelson Mandela) [8]

You can overcome that giant through Christ who strentheneth you.

"David majors in God. He sees the GIANT, mind you; he just sees GOD more so." (Max Lucado) [9]

You can overcome that giant through Christ who strengtheneth you.

"And Caleb stilled the people before Moses, and said, Let us go up at once, and possess it; for we are well able to OVERCOME it." (Caleb, Numbers 13:30, KJV)

Overcome that giant through JESUS who gives you the strength to do all things!

"The BIGGER they come, as long as GOD is fighting your battles, the FASTER they flee!" (J. D. Dixon, Sr.)

To help my sons overcome "giants," and their "fears," and to encourage them, I give them several golden nuggets, which I have now imparted to you. Yep. Today, it takes some serious baseballs to stand and face those big bad San Francisco GIANTS in your life!

But have you noticed that throughout this chapter I always referred to our sixth mysterious traveler as brave? Well guess what? A synonym for brave is "courageous." There will come a time when you have to unlatch the gate and unleash your inner matador; that will be the time when you must man-up against "the bull," who is symbolic of life's riskiest challenges, just like that champion matador during his suave dance with death. And from hereafter you will, for you have just been touched by little brother *Courage*, who is a fan of the Los Angeles Angels.

Now go and change the world. Show us what you can do with all of that courage. Teach, motivate, and challenge us to *"Unlatch, and Unleash"* our inner matador, so that we too can join you and do our part to help make this world a better place.

Congratulations in advance! Here come the beautiful flowers, raining down at your boots!

Let me ask you something. Have you yet observed that after every Traveler, the footsteps of an even more intriguing Traveler are manifested? If you found the previous six family members to be fascinating individuals, then Traveler number seven is most certainly about to rock your world!

BE THE THERMOSTAT

"He must increase, but I must decrease."

- St. John 3:30, KJV

An alarm sounds.

Everyone outdoors abruptly stops what they are doing. Then, they sprint towards the nearest shelter! Cruising vehicles make sudden U-turns, and then speed off in the opposite direction! A natural weather disaster will occur in approximately twenty-five minutes. Maybe less!

Meanwhile, a casually dressed gentleman is relaxing in his man cave, reclined on his ivory leather throne with his feet crossed, listening to Beethoven playing softly through the speakers of his surround sound system and reading the local newspaper while puffing away on a Cuban cigar. Obviously oblivious to the nerve-rattling alarm and the historic event that undoubtedly will be BREAKING NEWS on CNN, which will be taking place outside in the exact area where he humbly resides, the unaware gentleman studiously flips to the next page.

Twenty-four minutes later, Mount Matavanu, an active volcano on the Island of Savai'i in Samoa, begins to erupt! Suddenly, fire and smoke and ashes explode out of the mouth of the volcano! Then, a fiery avalanche of molten lava violently cascades down the red-hot mountain!

Amazing Grace, how sweet the sound, that saved a wretch like me.

I once was lost, but now I'm found. Was blind, but now I see. [1]

Oh yeah. I once was blind. Not physically blind, but mentally blind. I once was mentally blind, therefore, I could not see the possibility of myself ever becoming a better man, husband, father or friend. I once was blind, therefore, I could not see the possibility of myself ever becoming a better Christian. I once was mentally blind, therefore, I could not see the possibility of the reality that *all things* are possible with God, that are impossible with men.

When you are mentally blind, you cannot see yourself as "becoming." Consequently, when you are mentally blind, you can only see yourself as merely "being." Oh yeah. I once was blind…but now I see.

Not only was I mentally blind. I was simultaneously spiritually blind. I once was spiritually blind, therefore, I could not see that Satan had blinded my mind from the truth that God really and truly loves me, and that He had a specific purpose and a special plan for my life. I once was spiritually blind, therefore, I could not see that Satan had blinded my mind from the truth that God is worthy to be praised and worshipped in spirit and in truth, and that God desires to have a personal relationship with me, through His Son Jesus Christ. I once was spiritually blind, therefore, I could not see that Satan had blinded my mind from the truth that God wants to use me for His glory and the up-building of His kingdom, and that he wanted me to sincerely repent of my sins, wholeheartedly serve Him, and faithfully follow His Son Jesus. I once was spiritually blind, therefore, I could not see that Satan had blinded my mind from the truth that God desired to fill me with and baptize me in the Holy Ghost.

When you are spiritually blind, you cannot see how much God loves you, and how seriously He desires to have a personal, intimate, unbreakable, everlasting relationship with you. Consequently, when you are spiritually blind, you only see the pleasures of sin, the enticement of worldly riches and fame, and the selfish benefits of self-satisfaction, self-gratification, and self-indulgence. When you are mentally blind, you are automatically spiritually blind, and therefore, you are merely carnal and you are merely prideful. Oh yeah, I once was blind…but now I see!

Howbeit, on the flip side of that same coin, being "blind" can yet have its advantages. There is such a thing as being figuratively "color blind." In his famous "I Have a Dream" speech, the Rev. Dr. Martin Luther King, Jr. said,

"…I have a dream that my four little children will one day live in a nation where they will not be judged by the color of their skin but by the content of their character.

I have a dream today!

I have a dream that one day, down in Alabama, with its vicious racists, with its governor having his lips dripping with the words of 'interposition' and 'nullification' – one day right there in Alabama little black boys and black girls will be able to join hands with little boys and white girls as sisters and brothers.

I have a dream today!" [2]

This liberated mentally is a prime example of what it means to be figuratively "color blind."

When you are color blind, despite the truth that my chocolate complexion is perhaps seven or more shades darker than your vanilla complexion, you will, howbeit, treat me with respect, you will accept me just the way I am, and you will love me compassionately, as your brother. When you are color blind, despite the truth that there are perhaps fifty shades of black, of which the color of my skin is one, while the color of your skin is a little closer to the opposite end of the spectrum, you will, howbeit, trust me, you will honor me, and you will appreciate me, as your brother. When you are color blind, despite the truth that my ancestral family tree is rooted in Africa, and your ancestral family tree is rooted in Europe, you will, howbeit, support me, you will encourage me, and you will defend my civil rights when necessary…as your brother.

In God's eyes, we are all family!

In God's eyes, we are all related!

In God's perfect, color blind eyes, we are all one people!

There is no respect of persons with God. This self-explanatory truth informs me that God, being "color blind" Himself, sees *all* of us as being equal human beings, no race better than the other! What if Dorothy was a closed-minded racist? She and Toto never would have made it back home to Kansas! Think about that.

Has anybody seen my expensive pair of cool mirrored-lens sunglasses? I seem to have misplaced them somewhere. Well anyway, that's not all that important right now. What is important is how much longer it will be for all of us to become color blind, figuratively, and someday, somehow, someway be able to join hands with one another as sisters and brothers. Think about that.

Inside his humble abode, perfectly safe from all present harm and danger, the cool, calm, collected gentleman glances down at the time on his platinum and diamond Rolex (no knock-off!). He then folds up his newspaper, lays it on his mahogany coffee table, puts out his half-way smoked cigar in his porcelain ashtray, picks up his stereo remote controller and blasts the volume higher. He lays it back on his coffee table, and then sets his reading glasses down and picks up his $250 dollar Mirrored-lens Ray-Ban shades.

The floor of his peaceful lair is completely covered with mounds and mounds of mesmerizing Emerald stones!

Mount Matavanu is now completely covered with bubbling, streaming, scorching lava.

In the middle of the awakened volcano, the lava begins to slowly pull apart like an elegant satin curtain of a hit Broadway musical stage production! Then, perfectly safe from all present harm and danger, out steps…guess who? It is none other than the humble homeowner of Mount Matavanu! Yeah. You know who. That's right! That composed gentleman who is fond of Beethoven. Who else did you expect? The Great and Powerful Wizard of Oz?

After he steps out, the lava curtains close behind him. His journey begins. He strolls at a steady, brisk stomp, in and out deserted villages of Samoan Island. And with each footstep…the entire island vibrates!

Remaining islanders discretely peek at him from their windows as he stomps by their hut-houses. He exits the cluster of villages, then marches straight toward a mountain waterfall.

The stature of this robust Samoan citizen makes "The Rock" look like "J.J." on Good Times. This gentle giant stands an incredible seven foot seven inches tall, and weighs an incredible six-hundred and fourty-three pounds! All Dwayne Johnson rock-solid muscle! This hulk is incredible! He himself should be considered a mountain! A "human mountain!" But is he human? Good question, because his nimbus is of Another World.

His snow-white long wavy hair worn in a braided ponytail down to the middle of his back, he is casually dressed from head-to-toe in all white. Snow-white. He is stylish in his Springtime outfit – Fedora hat with an emerald green feather, short-sleeve linen dress shirt with matching linen slacks, and a pair of Louis Vuitton Slide Sandals protecting his white Louis Vuitton silk dress socks from all present harm and danger, wearing a cool pair of mirrored-lens shades and walking with a cool porcelain cane. Finally, he reaches his destination.

The middle of the waterfall begins to slowly pull apart, like an elegant satin curtain of a hit Tyler Perry play stage production. Then, once again, perfectly safe from all present harm and danger, the titanic titan steps out onto the beach shore…without a single drop of water on him!

"Can you feel the energy?"

This is something I say to make my cousin Emerald laugh. It is our own little inside joke that pertains to something hilarious that happened to me many years ago on a sidewalk in Harlem of Upper Manhattan, where she lives in The Big Apple. Every time we are together, and I say these words to her, "Hey Cuz? Can you feel the energy?" she just bursts out laughing until her eyes become watery. And I love it! Then, whenever she regains her NYC composure, she looks at me with this big beautiful smile and says, "Cuz? You are soooooo crazy!" Believe it or not, I get that a lot, everywhere I travel.

There is something worth taking a mental note of regarding the distinctive energy that emanates from the aura of a person with a meek and mild spirit. There is something worth capturing regarding the unique energy of a person with a meek and mild spirit. There is something worth studying and appreciating regarding the rare energy of a person with a meek and mild spirit. I propose to you the notion that there is something worth contemplating regarding the noticeable, remarkable, undeniably distinctive energy that effortlessly oozes out of the soul of a person with a meek and mild spirit.

A meek spirit is one human attribute that every living, breathing, mobile, sane human being in this world today should aggressively endeavor to attain! I mean, we aggressively pursue everything else that we want to achieve out of life, right? So why not aggressively pursue a spirit of meekness? We chase after that ever-so elusive million-dollar dream, career, and lifestyle daily, so why can't we also aggressively endeavor to attain a spirit of meekness?

Ponder this thought: As powerful as Jesus the Messiah was, and IS, He always, always, always maintained a spirit of meekness about Himself. Right?

When Christ turned water into wine, He kept His meek and mild spirit

When Christ successfully fasted for forty days and forty nights, then afterwards overcame the temptation of Satan, He kept His meek and mild spirit.

When Christ healed the impotent man who was sick for

thirty-eight years at the pool of Bethesda, He kept His meek and mild spirit.

When Christ cast out devils and demons with the power of His word, He kept His meek and mild spirit.

When Christ awakened and rebuked the wind and the raging sea and they obeyed His command and became calm, He kept His meek and mild spirit.

When Christ healed the woman with the issue of blood for twelve years when she touched the hem of His garment, He kept His meek and mild spirit.

When Christ healed the man who had a withered hand, He kept His meek and mild spirit.

When Christ fed five-thousand hungry people with only five loaves and only two fish, He kept His meek and mild spirit.

When Christ walked on the water of a raging sea, He kept His meek and mild spirit.

When Christ raised Lazarus from the dead, He kept His meek and mild spirit.

When Christ healed the lame, the blind, the dumb, and the maimed, He kept His meek and mild spirit.

When Christ was transfigured on a high mountain, He kept His meek and mild spirit.

And when Jesus was resurrected on that third day morning as the Risen Savior of the world, being victorious over death, hell, and the grave, with all power given unto Him in heaven and in earth, after taking the keys of Satan's kingdom, nevertheless, He *still* kept His spirit of meekness! Praise God! Let all of that digest. Delicious! Right?

Now, consider this conceptuality. Whenever you encounter an individual with a meek and mild spirit, you are left standing there in your spot, as if in a trance, feeling overwhelmed with a sense of self-reflection. Understand that the reason for this awkward internal somatesthesia is because most of us are so consumed with self that whenever our self-centered spirit encounters a spirit of meekness, we are literally forced to check ourselves. Or in other words, we are spiritually compelled to examine our own spirit. Thus, another term for this mental evaluation is "self-reflection."

Contrary to popular opinion, you and I are not one-hundred percent responsible for our self-centered mindset. We are victims of the "spirit of this age," the ungodly spirit of self-absorption, by which we are subliminally influenced. Our subconscious is deceived by none other than the spirit of the Enemy. Satan! So, until...

Standing with your eyes glued to your reflection in the mirror, you are suddenly snapped out of your trance by a strange vibration of your bathroom floor. Then, mysteriously, the puzzled reflection of yourself in the mirror disappears! Your eyes pop open as wide as your jaw has dropped! Then, a giant hand reaches through the mirror and a pointed finger touches you at the top of your chest, right above your heart.

Well? Here we are again. This is the part you have been patiently waiting for, at least up until this point. It is time to disclose the identity of the intriguing Traveler number seven. Are you bursting with anticipation?

Imagination is daring.

Faith is dedicated.

Gifted is delightsome.

Character is disciplined.

Wisdom is demanding.

Courage is determined.

And now, let us welcome to the stage the main attraction, the star of the show, the man of the hour...Mister Humility!!! Let's give him a standing ovation as he takes a bow. Big brother *Humility*...please allow me to rephrase that...BIIIIIIIG brother Humility is lucky number seven of our fascinating family of Travelers. And aren't we lucky! Despite the fact that he was born blind, without Humility, the rest of the seeing family members might as well have stayed home eating popcorn and watching Netflix. Correct? Excuse me? What was that? Oh? You didn't know Humility was blind? Aww man! Please don't tell me I forgot to mention that his newspaper was in braille? Sorry. My bad. Nonetheless, that Humility fellow, he is an angel of a guy!

We walk by faith, and not by our 20/20 vision.

Ponder this thought: If we could see into our future, why would we need to walk by faith? If we could see what obstacle is waiting around the corner for us, then why would we need to walk by faith? If we could see what lies ahead for us tomorrow, why would we need to walk by faith? If we could predict what is going to happen to us before our footsteps even guide us to the place of our prediction, then why would God need or want or have to order our steps in the first place? What would it matter? Why would it matter?

Lithuanian powerlifter and professional strongman Zydrunas Savickas currently holds three titles as the "World's Strongest Man." In 2014, he set a new world record at the Arnold Strongman Classic in the deadlift competition. [3] All he did was deadlift 1,155 pounds. That's all. For Big Z, it was just another day at the office. But the rest of us mere mortals, especially all of those spectators who were blessed to be able to witness this once-in-a-lifetime feat live and in person, celebrated this unreal historic event and went bananas!

On that day, Big Z almost literally brought the house down! One thousand, one hundred and fifty-five pounds is eight-hundred and forty-five pounds away from one ton! One ton? Who does that? Who goes around deadlifting over half a ton, as easy as lifting up a 9.6 pound baby boy? I'll tell you who. In the year 2014, it was six foot, three inches tall, three-hundred and seventy-five pound, Big Zydrunas Savickas, also known as "Big Z," from Lithuania. That's who!

And what about that "Human Lightning Bolt" who goes by the name of Usain Bolt? In the 2009 World Championships, Usain Bolt's all-time top speed broke the all-time world record. All he did was finish first in the one-hundred meter sprint with a recorded time of 9.58 seconds.

[4] Shucks. All he did was reach a speed of twenty-eight miles per hour. That was just another day at the office for him.

I bet his mind was elsewhere while he was coasting at twenty-eight miles per hour. He was probably thinking about if he remembered to turn the iron off before he left his hotel suite. Or perhaps he was wondering if that rookie valet driver took extra caution while parking his brand new Bugatti Chiron – the fastest, most powerful, and most expensive car in the world. Maybe, while he zipped by all of his so-called "competition," as if they were all running in slow-motion, his mind was wandering and he was daydreaming about enjoying some delicious Popeye's Louisiana Chicken! Mmmm, Mmmm, Mmmm. Finger-lickin' good! Whether his mind was here or there is inconsequential. Because you see, the rest of us mere mortals, especially all of those spectators who were blessed to able to witness this once-in-a-lifetime feat live and in person, celebrated this mindboggling historic event and lost our minds!

Now ponder this thought: If God chose to endow a man with the superhuman ability to deadlift 1,155 pounds, and chose to enable a man with the superhuman ability to sprint twenty-eight miles per hour, then why hasn't God ever chosen to empower at least one of us mere mortals with the superhuman ability to walk daily by clairvoyance, instead of having to rely on and trust in God and His Promises, and to "walk by faith, and not by 20/20 vision"?

Do you want to know what I think? I believe that God simply wants you and I, and all the rest of us mere mortals, to depend on His perfect wisdom, His perfect protection, His perfect goodness, His perfect mercy, His perfect provision, and His perfect favor *daily*. Most of all, I believe that God simply wants you and I to humble ourselves and depend on and accept His perfect love…*daily!*

Therefore, we mere mortals walk by faith, and not by a "crystal ball."

As quickly as it disappeared, your reflection reappears,

now expressing a sigh of relief!

Your sigh of relief turns into a grin. Your grin turns into a smile. Your smile turns into laughter! Then, you think aloud to yourself, "Wow! I am so glad my footsteps led me to this little book! Wow!"

"The steps of a good man are ordered by the LORD: and he delighteth in his way" (Psalms 37:23, KJV).

Understand that a humble spirit sets an atmosphere that changes everybody's attitude from bitter to better! Now that is what I call a "temperature regulator," ladies and gentlemen. There are two types of people in the world today. Thermometers, and Thermostats. Thermometers are those grumpy people who wait and wish for someone else to come along and create a better atmosphere. Thermostats, on the other hand, are the gentle ones who actually *change* the vibe with their meek and mild personality and their compelling humility; and thus, make all the Thermometers smile. And today, YOU have become a Thermostat!

Now go and change the world! Show us what you can do with your humble spirit. You have been touched by Mister Humility, the blind "Faith Walker." Therefore, you are now equipped with the power to regulate the mood of your environment. So…*Be The Thermostat!*

Congratulations in advance.

Mister Humility has not left the building! He is still trying to find the exit. However, another Traveler's footsteps are making their way up to the stage! But hey? Big brother Humility sure does have a mighty big pair of Louis Vuitton Slide Sandals to follow. So? Our eighth Traveler has got to be mighty amazing, if she is going to walk a mile in her forerunner's shoes. Because Humility is one tough act to follow. Think about it.

Oh yeah!

Humility is directive.

Despite the fact that he has difficulty finding his way off the stage.

LIKE THE TRANQUIL FLIGHT OF A DOVE

"He giveth power to the faint; and to them that have no might He increaseth strength.

Even the youths shall faint and be weary, and the young men shall utterly fall:

But they that wait upon the LORD shall renew their strength;

they shall run, and not be weary; and they shall walk, and not faint."

-     Isaiah 40:29-31, KJV

Are you still wearing your virtual reality goggles? Then let us ease on down that Yellow Brick Road. And don't you carry nothing, that might be a load. Let us ease on down, ease on down, down the road.

As you read these words, visualize them until they become alive, until they begin to breathe like you and I, until you are able to audibly hear this chapter's heartbeat. In order for you to fully engage and engross yourself in this story's journey, I encourage you to escape the boundaries of your brain. Escape the prison walls of logic, and simply dive off the crest of Mount Fuji. And while you are in freefall, spread your wings and soar like the mighty golden eagle. No. That was chapter four – *The Giants Giant*. Instead, while you are in freefall, spread your wings and glide like the graceful dove, until this story becomes tangible to you, until this story becomes virtual reality to you, until this story becomes *alive* to you!

Here we go. Jump!

The weather is fantastic. The North Carolina tar-heel blue skies are filled with cotton-white fluffy clouds and glistening golden sunshine. The astonishing arc of a heavenly rainbow arrests the attention of spectators who are blessed to be at the right place at the right time and witness this breathtaking marvel.

This rainbow is alive! You can feel his energy! You know he is watching you, as you are standing there staring up at him in awe!

Underneath the euphoric splendor of this rainbow stands the internationally famous Christ the Redeemer statue. This breathtaking, once-in-a-lifetime spectacle of a fascinating rainbow above the head of the equally marvelous ninety-eight-foot tall statue of the Messiah Jesus Christ on the peak of the two-thousand, three-hundred-foot-high Corcovado Mountain in Rio de Janeiro, Brazil, appears to be the glorious crown of King Jesus and is a mental image that you will remember forever. And I am sure big brother Imagination will be proud of you and I both for activating the power of our vivid imaginations. We might even have put a smile on that villainous, nefarious mug…I mean, on that charming face of his. He is such a swell guy.

Hundreds of selfie-taking tourists are crowded around the base of the statue's pedestal. The atmosphere is festive, and everyone's mood is overall celebratory. Echoes of laughter from a multitude of smiling faces overwhelm the soul with sheer happiness. The Tijuca Forest, home of the Corcovado Mountains that overlook the City of Rio, is a jaw-dropping vantage-point from which to view the world below.

Visually unnoticed, a woman simply dives off of an

unoccupied portion of Real Estate on the peak of the two-thousand, three-hundred-foot-high Corcovado Mountain, and freefalls head first to the world below.

Perhaps your jaw has dropped. But it's okay, everything is cool. You see, my friend, this is not her first rodeo. So, if this seemingly insane woman, who may have possibly escaped a nearby asylum and the "prison walls of logic," obviously survived this insane decision before, let us have the insanity of faith to believe she will somehow miraculously endure this flight also. Most "sane" people would choose to air travel by way of an airplane. This notion is difficult to dispute. However, this particular peculiar peril-embracing person is illogically yet immortally impervious to human fate. Therefore, she chooses air-travel…without the assistance of an airplane!

SHAZAM!

Ladies and gentlemen, this is the superhero I used to always imagine that I could fly like when I was a kid. To be honest with you, even today I wish I could fly high up in the sky just like SHAZAM. Don't laugh! If you were to be frankly honest and transparent too, I am sure that there is some comic book or fictitious silver-screen superhero whose superpowers you wish you had! I am not ashamed of the fact that I'm a golden-lightning-bolt type of guy.

You see, ladies and gentlemen, in my mind of creative genius and wild imagination, by day I am a humble, mild-mannered preacher and Christian Counselor. But at nightfall, I transform into my alter ego – a Black superhero with the same abilities as…SHAZAM! Oh? So, you are going to just sit there in your virtual reality googles, sipping on your favorite smoothie, and keep on laughing at me? Really, ladies and gentlemen? Like I am the only one who is running around at night fighting crime in a Halloween costume in their mind? Please.

But before you make that phone call and have me admitted to the nut house, ladies and gentlemen, at least allow me to plead my case, before you have me put in that nice cozy white straightjacket. It's like this…

Personally, "the Sky is the Limit" is more
than just a metaphor.
Double check your cape or your wings,
because if you try to follow me,
Ladies and Gents, Guys and Gals,
then you better soar!
And yes!
I'm standing on the Zenith,
the Apex, the Crest.
I wear the Golden Lightning Bolt
upon my chest
because I'm blessed!
So sport your Superman S,
or your Batman Bat Symbol.
I'm a Soldier for Jesus Christ,
therefore, I'm VICTORIOUS,
and it's that simple!
So sport your Superman S,
if that makes you feel fly.
Oh? Who am I?
Well, I'm a Golden Lightning Bolt
type of guy.

Still think I'm ready for the crazy house? Really? Wow.
Well give me one more chance. Thank you.

*"He giveth POWER to the faint; and to them that have no might
He increaseth strength.*

*Even the youths shall faint and be weary, and the young men shall
utterly fall:*

*But they that wait upon the LORD shall renew their strength;
they shall MOUNT UP WITH WINGS AS EAGLES; they
shall run and not be weary; and they shall walk, and not faint."*
(Isaiah 40:29-31, KJV)

Oh? Who am I?
Well, I'm a Golden Lightning Bolt
type of guy.

SHAZAM!

A cute little four-year-old Swedish girl, who sort of reminds you of one of your sweet little four-year-old nieces, is methodically brushing her Swedish Barbie Doll's long, straight blonde hair. Suddenly, she is distracted. She quickly looks up and gazes through the clear glass. Her jaw drops. Next, her beloved Barbie Doll drops. Waving and smiling at the awestruck little girl is a gorgeous middle-aged, ageless beauty from South America—from Brazil, to be precise.

The excited little girl turns and tugs on her napping mother's elbow, successfully interrupting her sweet dreams of being a victorious "Faith Walker," from being inspired by a little chapter book titled *The Traveler's Touch* that is lying on her lap. The half-dazed mother tries to concentrate and fine-tune her hazy perspective on the direction where her hysterical young daughter is frantically pointing her little finger. They both stare through the window at the Carolina blue skies, the cotton-white fluffy clouds, and the glistening golden sunshine. The shocked little girl's jaw drops a second time. Her "vision" has vanished.

As graceful as a dove, this vision of celestial enchantment enters and then exits massive cotton white fluffy clouds like one of God's beloved angels; an angel temporarily vacationing from her occupation and habitat up in the heavens, an angel disguised as a gorgeous middle-aged, ageless Brazilian beauty. As graceful as a dove, our eighth extraordinary Traveler glides throughout the endless sea of Carolina blue skies with outstretched arms and tight fists, with more grace than those fictitious heroines: DC Comic's Supergirl, and Marvel Comic's Ms. Marvel.

With your imagination now operating at maximum

capacity, you have to agree that this angel of a woman is as astonishing as the artistry of the arc of that rainbow over the head of the Christ the Redeemer statue!

Giving a fresh meaning to the phrase "The sky is the limit," this Super Marvel heroine-like woman gracefully glides above the clouds, through the stratosphere, from the continent of South America to the continent of North America. She is not wearing a sensuous spandex crime-fighting costume, including those subtly seductive knee-high stretch-leather high-heel boots, like Supergirl and Ms. Marvel and the long list of others alike. She is not even sporting the usual long heroic cape, but is dressed rather conservatively in business attire with chocolate waist-length blazer with matching slacks and high-heels. This is a business trip, and she is on a first class flight!

Finally, our eighth mysterious Traveler reaches her destination as the sun sets.

Again, visually unnoticed, which is a miracle within itself, she lands gracefully upon the sand of South Beach in Miami, Florida. She gracefully struts, in supermodel fashion, from the beach to a boardwalk, and then onward to the sidewalk and into the city's nightlife district. As her theme music from "Charlie's Angel's" plays in the background, she and her gorgeous sandy brown hair – braided and pinned-up in a tight bun – evaporate like a vapor in the midst of an inebriated, "off-the-chain" crowd of partying people.

DING DONG! Your doorbell rings. Still standing speechless, fixated on your reflection in your bathroom mirror, you release your grip from the sink and jog through your house to answer the front door. Unfortunately, there's no peephole in the door, so you eagerly open the door. No visitor. You extend your neck and peep your head outside, looking left, and then right. The scenery looks something like the scene in The Wonderful Wizard of Oz, when Dorothy was trapped inside of her farmhouse that was spinning inside that mean twister. Automobiles of all types are flying by! And so are your neighbor's pets; dogs and cats!

Howbeit, houses in your nice quiet neighborhood are flying by, zooming around your house! You shut and lock your door, then you begin to leisurely stroll back to your bathroom, thinking silently to yourself, *now that's strange*.

A perfect postcard sunset fades beyond the magical Atlantic Ocean off the coastal beaches of mystical Miami in The Sunshine State! On the flip side of that same coin, the Fahrenheit is stubborn and merciless, even at dusk, and refuses to budge from three digit temperatures.

Question: do you like paradise?

Paradise. Hmmm. That reminds me of a poem I wrote in my Poetry Collection Chapbook, entitled COME UP HITHER;

"Cruising down the street in my convertible Bugatti Veyron;
the Atlantic Ocean Summer Breeze caressing my face.
South Beach, Miami; definitely a Bucket List destination.
If you like Paradise, I'm sure you'll love this place..."

I'll ask again: do you like paradise?

That was too easy to answer. A no-brainer, as some would say. Well? I must say that I am sure you will love South Beach in Miami, if you have yet to experience this "paradise." In my modest opinion, it is definitely a bucket list destination!

And speaking of destinations, here is a good and predestined place in this chapter of our tale where I cease from prolonging the identity of this "fly girl," as some would say. So who is this mystery woman who loves to fly first class as her favorite choice of long-distance travel?

Here is your answer:

Standing a towering six foot, four inches tall without her chocolate Manolo Blahnik six-inch stilettos on, this statuesque head-turner, whose silky smooth bronze skin tone typifies the natural all-year tan of natives of beautiful Brazil, is definitely a bucket list sight to behold! Perhaps an

Olympic gold medalist beach volleyball champion in her younger days? Or perhaps a former professional runway model, strutting her "tail-feathers" on the catwalk? Or perhaps neither.

Nevertheless, her jaw-dropping stature, combined with her youthful essence and jaw-dropping good-looks, makes this middle-aged Super Marvel as equally fascinating as her brother Humility, who himself made quite a show stopping entrance and an impactful impression in your mental database. It does not appear that you will lose the memory of big sister Grace either…at least not anytime soon. Grace, traveler number eight, is ironically the equated epitome of her name – Grace. Just as that gorgeous ageless beauty Jaclyn Smith is synonymous with "Angel."

> She flies high up above,
> with the grace of a dove.
> Flying high up above,
> with both outstretched hands clutched.
> Her job assignment below,
> will forever be transformed by her touch.

Oddly, on your eighth footstep towards your bathroom—DING DONG—your doorbell rings! You snarl. You growl. You huff. This time, with immense impatience, you open your front door as forcefully as you slammed it shut the last time. Once again, no visitor. Once again, you peep outside and you look left-to-right, with a scowl of deep frustration written all over your face, of course. Now, with a temper as hot as the Miami heat, you slam your door shut, lock it, turn around and proceed to stomp toward your intended destination…again!

God is good.

If you are reading this statement right at this exact moment and you disagree that God is good, then check your pulse. Okay. Do you still have one? Ohhhh? You say you do still have a pulse, huh? Well, well. If you are somewhat like me, and have a past, and you know what kind of past I am talking about, and if your pulse is still functioning quite normally today, I think I feel pretty confident in saying that God has been good to you.

Okay then? Look at it from this angle. If God has not been good to you, then let me ask you this simple question, my friend: were you able to make your last Birthday? What do I mean? I will explain. On your last Birthday, whether it was last night, last week, last month, or last year, if you were present, then what that reveals to me is the fact that God was good enough to you to allow you the opportunity to see your last Birthday. And just in case you were wondering, the reason I capitalize the "b" in Birthday is because God is good enough to me, in that He has allowed ME the opportunity to make MY last Birthday! In other words, the reason I capitalize the "b" in Birthday is because of God's grace and mercy. I would have been gone a long time ago, but God spared my life; protected me from danger, harm and evil, kept my mind from going insane, and healed my ill and injured body, over and over and over again! Therefore, I am so grateful to God for blessing me see another Birthday, that I always capitalize the "b" to honor Him. And I don't know about you, but that is something I absolutely refuse to take for granted! So yes. God is good.

In fact, God is so good that He allowed you the opportunity to borrow a little bit of His oxygen this morning when you woke up and got out of bed; just enough air to keep your lungs properly inhaling and exhaling, all day long. No big deal. You are just living today, breathing today, alive today, enjoying God's "free oxygen" today. That's all. And if you really feel like being alive today, having breath in your body today, having the use and activity of all your limbs today, and being clothed in your right mind today is not really all that important of a reason to thank God today, and thus acknowledge that He is indeed a good God, then I guess you must be one of God's angels then, huh? But then again, you couldn't be an angel, because even the angels sing praises unto God in heaven…continually!

Allow me to make a suggestion. If you have never gotten into the habit of thanking God on a daily basis, or at the least on a regular basis, and thus acknowledging His goodness toward you, to your family, and to all of your loved ones, give it try. Yeah. Just give it a try every now and then. You know what? On second thought, if you will agree with me that God is good, and has been really good to you throughout the years, then I dare you to give God the praise He so deserves! God is worthy to be praised! God is worthy of thanksgiving! God is worthy of your Hallelujahs! God is just plain worthy, period! When I think of the goodness of Jesus and all that He has done for me, my soul cries out, "HALLELUJAH! I thank God for saving me!"

God is good, God is worthy to be praised, and God is deserving of our worship. And God particularly desires us to worship Him "in spirit and in truth." But as for you and I, God's human creations? Who are just dust? In whom no good thing dwells? Here is a news flash for you: BREAKING NEWS: "Hold up. Wait a minute. Okay. This report just came in. We human beings are not worthy of God's goodness. And furthermore, we human beings do not deserve any of God's goodness. This is mainly due to the fact that we are *all* as an unclean thing, and all of our righteousness is as filthy rags. For all have sinned, and come short of the glory God!"

To put it bluntly, we do not deserve the chance to borrow even a little bit of God's oxygen. And you may feel as if I am taking this a little bit too far. I can accept that. Yet we, you and I, will eventually utterly self-destruct, unless…

"Good Morning, So-and-So."

What is the result of the hand of the Almighty God being upon a person? Hmmm?

If there really is such a thing as a "million-dollar question," then this question is the answer to the question. And by that, I mean this: If you are fortunate to have at least an average IQ, let's say around a score of about one-hundred and seven, then it should be rather easy for you tell when a person is unparalleled. Well? What does it mean to be unparalleled? When it is quite obvious that a person is unparalleled, then it should be rather easy to see that this particular person is unique. Well? What does it mean to be unique? When it is quite obvious that a person is unique, then it should be rather easy to recognize that this particular person is incomparable. Well? What does it mean to be incomparable? When it is quite obvious that a person is incomparable, then it should be rather easy to identify that this particular person is extraordinary. Well then? What does it mean to be extraordinary? If your Intelligence Quotient is at least one-hundred, then it should be rather easy for you to tell when a person is functioning with the hand of the Almighty God upon them.

Still befuddled?

Okay then. Let us take another route.

How well do you function in life? Do you conquer your issues like a warrior? Or do you cower like a wimp? How well do you navigate through life? Do you overthrow your troubles like a great hero? Or do you rollover like a great zero? How well do you deal with problems in life? Do you grab them by the throat, then put them in the headlock, then lift them up over your head, and then body-slam them down onto the canvas? WHAM! Or does the opposite occasionally happen to you? WHAM!

The following information is the result of the hand of the Almighty God upon a particular person.

I personally like to refer to this mystical occurrence as the "Up, Up and Away!" appeal.

When a person is able to roller skate right over and across pandemonium, the hand of the Almighty God is upon them. When a person is able to do the electric slide right over and across uncertainty, the hand of the Almighty God is upon them. When a person is able to backstroke right over and across tribulation, the hand of the Almighty

God is upon them. And when a particular person is able to waterslide right over and across the tsunamis of life, even Stevie Wonder can see that the hand of the Almighty God is upon them, and thus, this particular person has the "Up, Up and Away!" appeal. And you know it! And I know it!

Faster than a speeding bullet!
More powerful than a locomotive!
Able to leap tall buildings in a single bound!
Look? Up in the sky!
It's a bird!
It's a plane!
No. It's…
It's that person with the Hand of the Almighty God upon them!

UP, UP…and AWAAAAaaaay!!!
"Good morning, So-and-So. My name is *Grace*."
She reaches out to shake your hand. You shake her hand, and then you faint. Now that is what I call one power-packed potent handshake! Do Brazilians usually have a grip of this magnitude? Maybe they do? I don't know. And I'm not so sure that I would like to find out. I like these fingers. I find them to be very useful. In fact, a couple of them helped me write this book.

Yes. You have fainted. There is no need to panic though. You are in good hands, despite that Supergirl handgrip of hers. Big sister Grace has deposited something inside of you, through the awesome touch of her handshake, that is going to transform your life forever, whenever you wake up…again. And whenever you do wake up, you will be empowered with grace that is *Like the Tranquil Flight of a Dove*. Your grace upon grace will empower you to accomplish EVERYTHING that you otherwise normally would NOT be able to achieve without the aid of God's Amazing Grace!

Big sister Grace is an amazing Amazon. Simply

enthralling! And she has just supernaturally transferred the grace that is on her life onto your life, through the invisible gateway inside your palm. Even as you are reading these words—words that are *alive*, words that are breathing like you and I, words that have a heartbeat that you can audibly hear—Grace's touch of grace is traveling throughout every atom that connects to form molecules, which connect to form your molecular makeup! After conceptualizing this mind-blowing concept, you will eventually accept the idea that Grace's supernatural transference of grace into your being is just as amazing as the actual live event of witnessing the astonishing arc of a heavenly rainbow over the head of the most spectacular statue in the whole world – the Christ the Redeemer stature in Rio de Janeiro, Brazil.

Along with India's Taj Mahal, Mexico's Chichen Itza, Rome's Coliseum, China's Great Wall, Peru's Machu Picchu, and Jordan's Petra, Brazil's Christ the Redeemer Statue is recognized as one of the new Seven Wonders of the World. And just like the tranquil flight of a dove, the Amazing Grace by which you will "glide in," will likewise be recognized as a Wonder of the World!

South Beach, Miami;
definitely a Bucket List destination.
If you like Paradise,
I'm sure you'll love this place.
But oh, there is absolutely no place
I would rather be,
than abiding in the center of the Palm
of God's Amazing Hand of Grace.

Thank you. I appreciate that. And I hope you appreciate how I changed-up and threw a curve ball with big sister Grace's method of transportation. Big brother Humility sure does have a mighty big pair of sandals to follow. So? Our eighth Traveler has got to be mighty Amazing if they are going to walk a mile in their forerunner's shoes.

Remember that? Gotcha! And mighty amazing big sister Grace is. Obviously, her virtue is of Another World.

Here is some "Soup for the Soul":

Keep on living, and someday you will find yourself at the most fragile, the most vulnerable, the most down-and-out, the lowest, the weakest point of your life. I have been there. Live long enough, and so will you. But, do not be discouraged.

"And He [Jesus] said unto me, 'My grace is sufficient for thee: for MY STRENGTH is made perfect in weakness…'" (II Corinthians 12:9, KJV)

Today, my friend, if you are experiencing a considerable degree of depression, disappointment, discouragement, or defeat, and consequently, you are feeling weaker than the weakest you have ever felt, remember this: have no fear, because the Amazing Grace of God is here to uphold you in the palm of His Mighty Hand! Now, if this is not a spoken word of encouragement, then, after all of these years as a preacher and Christian Counselor, I have yet to speak it. So, receive it…in Jesus' name.

Now go and change the world. Show us what you can do with your amazing grace. You have been touched by the hand of Grace. Literally. Therefore, from now on the grace in which you will "glide" will have multitudes of selfie-taking addicts speechless and spellbound, standing and staring at you in amazement. And guess what? The grace upon grace which you will abide in will be accredited for being the inspiration that set ablaze a fire that motivated your crowd of selfie-takers to put away their smartphones, and to stir-up their dormant dreams and begin to pursue them once again!

From this day forward, you are a faith-walking "Walking Inspiration"!

Congratulations in advance.

Eight down. Two to go. I don't know about you, but right at this moment, I am downright pumped-up about meeting our next terrific Traveler with a triumphant touch!

Will they arrive by foot?
Will they arrive by vehicle?
Will they arrive by boat?
Will they arrive by airplane?
With just a turn of a few pages,
we will soon find out.
But however they choose to reach us,
and however they choose to touch us,
our lives will NEVER be the same.

Didn't quite rhyme, but, I gave it a shot anyway.

I sat down in the chair next to her, leaned over and rested my arms on the rail of her bed. "What's your name?" I asked.

PURPOSE-DRIVEN PURPOSE

"For as we have many members in one body, and all members have not the same office:

So we, being many, are one body in Christ, and every one members one of another.

Having then gifts differing according to the grace that is given to us,

whether prophecy, let us prophesy according to the proportion of faith;

Or ministry, let us wait on our ministering: or he that teacheth, on teaching;

Or he that exhorteth, on exhortation: he that giveth, let him do it with simplicity;

he that ruleth, with diligence; he that showeth mercy, with cheerfulness."

- Romans 12:4-8, KJV

SLAM!
Your fallen house has finally reached its destination. Shaken up by the jolting collision against the ground, you are immediately awakened out of your peaceful snooze and brought back to Mother Earth. You pop-up off your pillow

like a human Pop-Tart. You scurry over to your bedroom window, which is now a hole in the wall, literally. As you gaze out into the wild blue yonder in absolute fascination, you absolutely cannot believe what your eyeballs are witnessing!

You step outside through your front door, which is now an even bigger hole in the wall, and just stand in awe. You ask yourself an unanswerable question: "What in heaven's name is this place?" The sky is the color of pink lemonade. The humongous cotton white clouds give you the foolish impression that they are all staring down at you – a stranger in their land, a mysterious Traveler who has invaded their unimaginable world. While your attention is captivated by these "sky guardians," who do not appear as if they'll let you out of their sight anytime soon, from the corner of your left eye you catch a brief glimpse of the tail-end of something darting past you. And whatever it was, it is gone! Fast as greased lightning! Nope, even faster. Fast as a golden lightning bolt! It doesn't get much faster than that!

As you recall the memory of that awkward fist-bump touch from little brother Courage, you take a leap of faith and boldly bunny-hop off your front stoop. About a hundred feet away in the plush emerald green pastures, it appears as if two adult male unicorns are playfully jousting each other with the lone horn protruding from their foreheads. Suddenly, they freeze in mid-motion. They have spotted an intruder – you! And now their eyes are deadlocked on you, as you stand there stiff as a statue, as if you had just spotted a spotted unicorn off in the not-so-far distance. This anomaly has you stunned!

A flock of graceful, gliding doves add zest to the tranquil pink lemonade sky. Your bewildered eyes follow these delightsome fowls as they zig-zag through the fresh, poppy-scented air. You are utterly distracted. That is when…

"Hey you!"

Your head spins, and you locate the owner of this yelling voice. Levitating in mid-air, with no strings attached, not too high above your head and to your right, floats a sight that one could only try to imagine in ones dreams. So, you attempt to convince yourself: "So-and-So? You must be dreaming." Having read your mind and perceiving your thoughts, this mesmerizing, mystical, mythological madame, who is the spitting image of the one-and-only Miss Patti LaBelle, is all frowned-up and pointing her magic wand right at you!

This Divine Diva is sparkling from head to toe! Her silver crown is diamond-studded. Her silver Vera Wang sequin evening gown is completely embroidered with diamonds. Her silver Jimmy Choo high-heels are custom designed with diamonds. Her silver magic wand is decorated with diamonds. Her fingernails are sparkling like diamonds. Even her eyeshadow is sparkling like diamonds! And as you stand mystified and star struck, gazing upward at this distinguished Divalicious Diva, you cannot avoid thinking of the last time you enjoyed yourself a slice of delicious sweet potato Patti Pie! You point at your chest.

"Who? Me?"

"No! I'm talking to my two pet unicorns. Of course I'm talking to you, Silly! And you have the nerve to stand there and act all innocent, like you don't even realize that you are in some big trouble. I'm talking about some deep doo doo!"

"Big trouble? I'm in deep doo doo? Who, me? But why? What did I do? I just got here! Wherever here is."

"Well, let me enlighten you. First of all, here, where you are standing, is the Land of Zo. Second of all, you have entered our secret realm, our hidden domain, unannounced, uninvited, and personally unwelcomed. And third of all, you low-down, dirty, trifling Traveler, you are wearing my recently killed baby brother's favorite pair of thick red comfy thermal socks! And that is why you are in some deep, deep, deep doo doo, Silly! Now, take them off! And give them to me! NOW!"

Frightened, you look down at your favorite pair of thick red comfy thermal socks. You almost surrender to the demanding Diva's threatening demand. Then, a thought hits you. As you are about to obey this deranged Diva's intimidating request, you pause, you raise back up, and you boldly look her in her devilish diva eyes.

"Now, you wait a minute! Now it's your turn to listen to me yell at you, Madame Queen Diva! First of all, my name is not Silly. It's So-and-So! Second of all, I am not some kind of trifling Traveler! And third of all, Madame Mentally-Disturbed Diva, these comfy red socks are NOT coming off of my feet! NEVER!"

Then, you stick your chest out, lift your chin up, fold your arms, and bite down on your bottom lip like Muhammad Ali. And now, you are feeling like a boss! Literally!

"Oh no you didn't! You jive turkey burger! Now you've done REALLY went and ruffled my wings!"

Furious, with steamy fumes rising from her crown, literally, she forcefully aims her magic wand at you. Your eyes pop open! Then suddenly, that lightning fast whatchamacallit darts by you again! Next, Her Highness the Madame Queen Diva's eyes pop open!

In another realm, Queen Elizabeth, the Queen of England, is smiling. This means ALL of England will be happy. Her mind is at ease. Her heart is filled with peace. She has just had an important meeting with her Royal Advisor, which is a fancy name for personal consultant. A more fitting job title is personal counselor.

The Royal Advisor to the Queen of England is an employee of the Royal Buckingham Palace. She is such an asset to the Queen of England, that she resides at her own private wing inside the Royal Windsor Castle. This is no doubt the Queen's brilliant idea to keep her personal counselor nearby, in time of unforeseen crisis.

However, her services are not confined nor contained within the four walls of her Majesty's two Royal London-based Estates. Well, eight walls. The reputation of her special talent has proceeded her and has spoken loudly for itself, thus, her rare skills are sought after by royal dignitaries all over the globe.

Kings and queens, princes and princesses, dictators and dukes, ambassadors and archbishops, presidents, and even the Pope himself are blowing up her cellphone on a regular basis. Her smartphone is like an American Express Card…she doesn't leave home without it!

The Royal Advisor calls lovely London home. She is the only person in the history of human existence who is fluent in all six-thousand, five-hundred documented and official languages in the world today. Therefore, London, with all of her diverse cultures and ethnicities, is a suitable headquarters for Queen Elizabeth's trusted and loyal homegirl. Hold up! That's her cellphone ringing now. It's Queen Oprah on the other line.

Recently notified of her latest job assignment, this VIP is assisted up into her royal horse carriage, and then off she goes! Her trusted and loyal source of transportation – a team of four Clydesdale horses along with her driver – has been her source of transportation since the stagecoach was first invented in England in the 13th Century. Before that, she simply rode her favorite trusted and loyal black Shire horse, a gentle giant named Ambition.

Obviously, she is not a Girl Scout anymore. Nonetheless, that has not hindered her purpose over the past generations of providing direction to the lost, acting as a compass to the clueless, and bringing sight to the mentally and spiritually blind. Now you see why so many VIPs all around the world are blowing up her cellphone daily!

Sixteen hoofs of four strong, speedy stallions kick up dust, dirt, gravel and ground, as they steadfastly stride at a steady pace to make sure their royal owner is on time for her scheduled divine appointment. After racing over bridges, splashing through creeks, muscling up hillsides, dashing downward into dark valleys, the very important purpose-driven traveler finally reaches her destination.

A supernatural glow emanates from her aura. She sort of

reminds one of the legendary actress Della Reese, particularly when she played in the hit TV series "Touched by an Angel." Her vigor, vibrancy, and vitality is misleading, and does not at all match the multiple years of her longevity. Considering that our noble ninth Traveler is originally a Native of the Andaman Islands and thus a Native of Great Andamanese, the oldest tribe of Africa, I would suggest that "longevity" is a most befitting word to characterize her physical appearance.

Remarkably, she is as light on her feet as her youngest daughter Gifted, our third "lead-foot" traveler. To prove my point, before her stagecoach driver even has the opportunity to assist her down from out of the carriage, after he opens her door she hops effortlessly onto both feet, as nimble as a Girl Scout. Thus, her exuberance is of Another World.

The Royal Traveler is fittingly fashionable, dressed in royal purple from head-to-toe. Her majestic wardrobe consists of a diamond-studded Queen Nefertiti crown upon her head, floor-length silk gown with matching diamond-studded sandals, and a solid gold Queen's Scepter, which is gripped tightly by her right hand. Mysteriously, the mysterious monarch steps into a mysterious realm, another realm, another dimension, perhaps into Another World. POOF! Gone. Like magic.

Like this purpose-driven Traveler, I was born to be successful for God's glory.

I know you may think to yourself that this is a rather arrogant confession. Though it may seem like a lofty, egotistical, bold and puffed-up presumption of myself, I know that I know that I know that I was born to be successful for God's glory.

In mid-May of 2014, as an early Father's Day gift, my beautiful wife – my Queen, my Rib, my Help Meet, my Highly Anointed Woman of God, my Good Thing – blessed me and purchased for me a shower gel which came with a sample bottle of cologne called "One Million," by

Paco Rabanne. And trust me, after I get myself fresh and clean with this shower gel called "One Million," I step out of my house smelling like a million bucks! And you can take that to the bank! Now watch this, not only do I *smell* like a million bucks when I step out of my house, I also *look* like a million bucks! And not only do I *look* like a million bucks when I step out of my house, but I also *feel* like a million bucks! That's right! I said it! I smell like MONEY! I look like MONEY! And I feel like MONEY! In Jesus' name! How? Why? I already told you. I was born to be successful for God's glory.

Whatever you think in your heart concerning yourself, that is what you will become.

Thus, I was born to be successful.

Whatever you think in your heart concerning your life, that is what will become of your life.

Thus, I was born to be prosperous.

Whatever you think in your heart concerning your future, that is what will become of your future.

Thus, I was born to be a blessing to many.

Whatever you think in your heart concerning your destiny, that is what will become of your destiny.

Thus, I was born to change lives…for the glory of God.

What I am trying to get you to see and stop and think about, is that YOU too are born to be successful at achieving something for God's glory! Yes. That's right! I said it! You too are born to be successful, born to be prosperous, born to be a blessing to many, and you too are born to change lives…for the glory of God. How? Why? Well, you already know the answer to these questions.

Listen. There are three bona fide "signposts" that will point you in the direction of your destiny, and thus reveal to you exactly what you are born to do.

1. Whatever issue that makes you storming mad! A problem that you feel passionately about and want to fix!

2. Whatever you cannot seem to stop dreaming about! An undying, undiminishing, undefeatable ambition!

3. Whatever comes naturally to you that most people find extremely difficult! A special "gift" which can only come from God of Heaven!

Listen. These golden nuggets are free, from me to you. No charge. So? Do not waste them!

Do you know why some people, no, scratch that, why hundreds of people are miserable and fed-up with their life today? I am not alluding that this is the gospel. I myself basically choose to believe, nonetheless, that a considerable amount of people all over the world today are unhappy and are barely surviving without any joy whatsoever in their life, is basically because they have not the slightest clue as to why they exist; nor why they are still here. They do not know their calling. Oh? What is a calling? I'll tell you.

Calling: "a strong desire to spend your life doing a certain kind of work, such as religious work; also, the work that a person does or should be doing." [1]

Truthfully speaking, deep down on the inside, everybody – whether Black or White, Brown or Bronze, rich or poor, politician or pimp, virtuous woman or video vixen – would honestly love to know that there is something more to life than what their life is currently offering.

Knowledge of self is a very powerful motivator! The real reason countless authors have generously contributed their copyrighted literary works to bookstores worldwide on this specific topic, is because the outcome is usually mutually rewarding. Readers become joyfully rich in self-discovery and authors become joyful during the monsoon season of royalty checks. And so goes the circle of life.

Any Holy Ghost-filled, fire baptized, born-again Believer will probably tell you that before they accepted Christ and then developed a genuine relationship with God the Father, their life was meaningless, moody, and miserable! Hopefully you as well can attest to this: Christians are very rich people; rich in imagination, rich in faith, rich in gifts, rich in character, rich in wisdom, rich in courage, rich in humility, rich in grace, and happily rich in "knowledge of self"! So basically, we Christians are a happy people because we have the Lord Jesus Christ in our lives, and therefore we KNOW why WE exist! And therefore, WE KNOW why we are still here. Praise God!

Now, I said all of that to say this: What about your destiny? Hmm? What is destiny?

Destiny: "a power that is believed to control what happens in the future." [2]

That, ladies and gentleman, is what I mean by destiny. And what about your calling? Are you not starving for the realization that there is more to life than what life is currently offering you?

Or are you completely satisfied, completely fulfilled, completely overjoyed with not knowing the divine "job assignment" that God actually created YOU to accomplish?

Yes. I guess you could say that what I am trying to say is, reaching your destiny and fulfilling your calling is so significant to El Shaddai, that He oftentimes generously deposits "libraries of books" within the heads of authors expounding and exhorting on the subject of "Reaching Your Destiny," and "Fulfilling Your Calling." So basically, until…

POOF!

"Wake up, So-and-So. It is time to rise and shine, my child."

Meanwhile, you are snoring and sound asleep in the fetal position like a cute little baby, sucking your thumb with a tickled grin on your face. Big sister Grace tucked you in bed, then whispered "sweet dreams" in your ear. This explains that tickled grin on your face. Pardon me? What was that? Oooooh? What about your job? What about school? Oh. I am quite confident that all of your concerns will be well taken care of by the end of the final chapter of this book.

Your eyes pop open! Instantly, you are awake. Just like magic! But hey? You are confused, not sure if you are stuck in the fantasy world of The Wonderful Wizard of Oz, now waking up and looking at Glinda, the Good Witch of the South. What is more important is that she came to your rescue just in the nick of time! This Good Queen Mother purposely woke you up seconds before the evil Madame Queen Diva could sink her divalicious fingernails deep into you, and commence to ripping you apart; limb by limb! That's right, this motherly Good Queen whom you refer to as "Glinda," snatched you from the clutches of that dastardly diva – Madame Queen Diva – when she woke you up!

"Who…?"

"Shhhh. It is not who, my little darling. It is when."

Oh yes. Now you are really discombobulated.

"When? When what? And how did you…? And where…? Where did you come…?"

"Shhhh. No more questions, for now. Happy birthday, my child. I have a present for you."

"Happy birthday? But? Today is not…Wait?"

You sit up in bed. Your undivided attention has at last been arrested.

"You said you have a present for me?"

You fight to contain a breakout happy-face smile. She chuckles.

"Yes, my love. Today is the first day of your when."

When was the last time you took the time to thank God for your "when"? Never? For real? Alright. When was the last time you took the time to analyze your "when"? What? Never? Wow. I must say, I am shocked. That is really hard for me to believe. What this reveals to me is just how "spiritual" you really are. Anyway. Put away all electronic devices – Smartphones, Ipads, Tablets, Smartwatches, etcetera. Strap on your thinking cap. Class is now in session.

My philosophy on the hypothesis of "When:"

W – Where?

H – Here.
E – Eternity.
N – NOW!
Shall I proceed? I thought you might say that.
When I step into the room it's like KABOOM!

1.   …Because I am living in the moment of my *when*.
     Therefore, my *when* says to me that your spirit-man
     – the real you, the unseen you – has supernaturally
     invited my presence into your presence because,
     unbeknownst to you, your future is predicated on
     my supernatural "connection" to you. Thus,
     KABOOM!

When I step into the room it's like KAPOW!

2.   …Because I am embracing the moment of my *when*.
     Therefore, my *when* says to me that right here, right
     now, is when the heavens are opening up, and
     pouring out the blessings of God upon and into my
     life. Thus, KAPOW!

When I step into the room it's like KABAM!

3.   …Because I am my *when*, and my *when* is who I am.
     Therefore, my *when* says to me that whenever I
     arrive at my predestined destination, it is at this
     precise moment of déjà vu in my life, from which
     my future will explode with brightness. Thus,
     KABAM!

Class is dismissed. No homework.

Then, Queen Mother Purpose leans forward and kisses
you on your forehead. All of a sudden, her cellphone rings.
POOF! Gone. Just like magic.

Delighted and disoriented at the same time, you fling the
cover and sheets off your body. THUD! Something solid,
something with a little weight falls off your bed and hits the
floor. You bend over and pick it up. You blurt out, "It's
Glinda's magic wand!" On the surface it appears as though
her Royal Highness has rushed-off and forgot her Royal
Queen's Scepter. Or did she intentionally leave it behind for
you? Like breadcrumbs in the Classic Fairy Tale Hansel and

Gretel?

You stand up. You notice you are barefooted and not wearing your socks! These were not just any ole pair of socks! These were your favorite pair; your thick red comfy thermal socks! Normally, this would not be a big deal, but...you cannot remember taking them off!

Oh well? Anyway, you examine the interesting metal rod in a state of utter bewilderment. And then, for some strange reason, you decide to point it as if aiming it at a stationary target. The floor trembles! The walls shake! All shook-up, you think aloud to yourself, "EARTHQUAKE!" All of a sudden, a mysterious portal opens right before your eyes! It is another realm, another dimension...perhaps it is another world. For some strange reason, you decide to cautiously step inside of this black hole. POOF!

Did you really want to know what was on the other side that badly?

Purpose-driven, you boldly stepped into nothingness. Or could have been just plain ole stupidity. Nevertheless, purpose-driven, our ninth VIP Traveler completed her job assignment. And her royal golden scepter is not your birthday present, but nice try.

It was her kiss on your forehead! Her name is...*Purpose*. And, that is what she gave you, *"Purpose-driven Purpose."*

When Baby Sis Gifted kissed you on your right cheek, you were miraculously endowed with that "special gift" you have. But, when Mother Purpose leaned forward and kissed you on your forehead, you were enlightened to what your "job assignment" is, enlightened to your purpose. Today is the first day of your "when." Today is the first day that you will begin to walk in your divine calling.

Understand that your Imagination, your Faith, your Gift, your Character, your Wisdom, your Courage, your Humility, and your Grace, all point to your Purpose! So, once again...happy birthday! What was that, my friend? What is your purpose? Shhhh. Like Mother Purpose said, no more questions, for now.

Now, go and change the world, my child. Show us what you can do with your purpose-driven purpose, your job assignment. I just showed you mine, my little darling. That's right! There you go! Climb up into the saddle of your black Shire horse, a gentle giant named Ambition, and pursue your purpose with passion!

Congratulations in advance!

Well? We are finally here. The final chapter. Wait? Let me try that again, because I don't think you caught it. The final chapter. FINALLY! Finally, we have reached our final destination. You and I. Together.

Let us review.

First, you were touched on your stomach.

Next, you were touched on your right cheek.

Then, you were touched on your left cheek.

Then, you were touched on your right shoulder.

Next, you were touched on your face.

Next, you were touched on your fist.

Then, you were touched on the top of your chest, right above your heart.

Next, you were touched on your palm, with a friendly-but-firm handshake.

And then, you were touched on your forehead, with a kiss, by a Queen.

Nine different extraordinary Touches.

Nine different extraordinary Travelers.

Nine different extraordinary Traits…supernaturally deposited into YOU!

Ponder this thought:

A family of eight Sensational Siblings, and one Magnificent Mother – a Majestic Mother whose name is Purpose! Wow! I cannot seem to stop smiling. I am smiling for you, on your behalf, my love. Okay. Okay. I'll stop. Just having a little fun. Hold up! I hear footsteps. Yes? More footsteps. Shhhh. No questions. Remember? I think it is a good idea if you and I were both still and quiet. Let's listen.

FINAL DESTINATION

"And now abideth faith, hope, charity, these three; but the greatest of these is charity."

- I Corinthians 13:13, KJV

There is an angry storm outside. Thundering and lightning and windy and hailing and raining felines and canines!

"Wow. It is really dark in here. And kind of spooky too. Hello? Is anybody home? It's me, So-and-So!"

No reply. The silence is just as eerie as the darkness.

"Hello? Good Witch of the South Glinda? I believe I'm ready to return back home to Kansas now! There's no place like home. There's no place like home. There's no place…awww this is silly. Probably won't work anyway. There's no place like home. Man! Told ya. I'm still here. Your Majesty? Somebody was blowing up your cellphone, and you rushed off and left your magic wand! And I'm only here to return it to you! So, are you in here? Queen Glinda? Where are you? Uuugh! I wish she would have told me her name. Wait a minute…maybe if I point this magic wand like this, over here in this direction, something will happen."

Approximately ten seconds later, POOF! The white lights are bright! Almost blinding.

"Hey? Where am I? What kind of room is this? Looks familiar," you think aloud to yourself. And then it hits you. "Hey? This is a patient's room in a hospital! Wait a minute?

This is ICU! But? Why am I here? Hold up. There's something very peculiar going on here. Somebody is playing some serious games with me. Why and how am I floating in air and looking down from the ceiling? Nah. This prank is not funny to me at all. And frankly, I'm starting to get…Hey? There's a patient down there, lying in bed, asleep."

Unfortunately, this patient is lying in a rather deep sleep…a coma. The patient is dying, with roughly six months to live. He is hooked up to a respirator but, fortunately, the activity shown on the monitor gives positive signs of hope. His vital organs—lungs, brain, heart—are clinging to precious life, as if God is buying time for the patient, waiting to see if he wants a second chance to live or if he is ready to die.

Do I know this patient? you wonder to yourself.

It appears to the natural human eye that you and the dying patient are the only two living souls in this hospital room. There is a peculiar chill in the room. The atmosphere is filled with a heavy sense of gloom and doom. Not overwhelming, but heavy. However, what is overwhelming is that gut feeling you are experiencing right now, a melancholy emotion that you are struggling to avoid. But your resisting is futile. Your premonition cannot, and will not be denied.

You know what is coming. Let me rephrase that. You know *who* is coming. You know they are approaching. And you know that when they arrive at their destination, which is here in this hospital room, in ICU. Their purpose is to do what they have come to do, to complete their job assignment. Now, you realize nobody is playing games with you and trying to pull a prank on you. So, you wave the white flag and clear your throat.

"Excuse me. Hey? You down there? Can you hear me? If you can, could you try to wiggle your finger for me?"

Suspended in air with your back just a few centimeters

from the ceiling, you strain with every fiber within you to focus your 20/20 vision on all ten of the comatose patient's lifeless fingers. Seconds pass. Minutes pass. Half an hour passes. According to the clock on the wall, which you are hoping is broke, two whole hours have passed! Still, no movement. No response from the patient. Not even the slightest wiggle of one pale finger. Then, painfully perplexed, you ask yourself, "Wait a minute? I just thought about it. Where in the world is the bleep bleep nurse? Is anybody in this crazy hospital going to come and check on this poor dying patient? Any time before the Rapture?"

Out of reasonable frustration, you aim Mother Purpose's royal queen's scepter down towards the patient, as if you seriously expect something magical to instantly happen. Then all of a sudden, you notice something else familiar. Instantaneously, that gut feeling travels back to your memory. You think you hear footsteps. No, it is just your imagination. Wait. Yes! You do hear footsteps. No! You don't. Yes. No. Yes! No. Your mind is the one playing serious games with you now, trying to pull a prank on you.

"I know that patient. That patient…is…"

You are momentarily speechless, as water quickly floods your eyes. Needless to say, your 20/20 vision has rapidly diminished. As soon as your agonizing mind grabs hold of reality, one tear after another begins to drip down onto the sleeping patient's face. It is important to mention that instead of immediately getting angry at the Lord up in Heaven above and cursing His Holy Name like most human beings in the same situation would do, you surrender to God's will, and attempt to cope with what seems to be your "Final Destination" in perhaps the near future. But you are not sure, so you reluctantly ask yourself a final question.

"I'm dying. How much time do I have left?"

Like I said, the patient has roughly six months to live; add or subtract a few days.

But what if you only had twenty-four hours left? Only twenty-four hours of breath left in your body. And then, it's curtains. The fat lady is on the stage singing her song. Goodnight. The show is over. The end. Roll the credits. No part two. No sequel. No non-fiction epic comeback-story drama.

Only twenty-four hours left.

Only twenty-four hours of goodbyes left.

Only twenty-four hours of farewells left.

Only twenty-four hours of tears of hope left.

Only twenty-four hours of tears of dread left.

Only twenty-four hours of suffering left.

Only twenty-four hours of fame & fortune left.

Only twenty-four hours of I'm sorry left.

Only twenty-four hours of I love you left.

Only twenty-four hours of you will see me again in Heaven left.

Only twenty-four hours left before you look around and find yourself in the place that is in the opposite direction of Heaven.

The greatest possession you have, the greatest gift you have, the greatest miracle you have, is the twenty-four hours directly in front of you! I often say it's getting late in the evening, and the sun is going down. In other words, while the clock is steadily ticking, life is steadily making preparations for its exit, for its final destination. However, this book is not about the afterlife. This book is about your life today. Therefore, I asked the question: What if you knew you had only twenty-four hours left?

Twenty-four hours.

Tall deep-rooted trees are uprooted by an unseen unnatural evil claw, one-by-one. This invisible foe lifts heavy-duty trucks, minivans, SUVs, and sedans into the air with ease and then drop the vehicles upside-down onto the asphalt, one-by-one. As this invisible menace marches up the street, roofs of attractive split-level homes are peeled off like an overworked Band Aid, one-by-one.

Finally, the angry storm has reached his final destination! One-by-one, golf ball-size hail bombard already destroyed automobiles and damaged houses. One-by-one, live powerlines unloosen and fall to the soaked cement, as telephone poles snap like breadsticks. You are home alone still wearing your favorite old, raggedy, torn Pittsburgh Steelers pajamas. You're on your knees in the proper elementary school safety position, trembling in terror and praying fervently and effectually. Suddenly, all of your windows are shattered, then sucked out. Guess where you are now? Unfortunately, yes. In the eye of an angry F4 Tornado! With insane wind-speeds of two-hundred and sixty miles per hour! Two hundred and sixty reasons for you to call on the Name of Jesus more intensely!

As your aching body is balled-up in your bathtub, terrified by this treacherous trial of tribulation, you continue to pray even more relentlessly, even though this psychotic cyclone is relentlessly attempting to murder your psyche. The combination of this deadly spinning funnel cloud in which you are helplessly imprisoned, along with the now ghostly quietness, is enough to drive anybody storming mad!

However, it is a good thing that today you still have your sanity. Yes, today you are in your right mind. Today you have a sound mind, a strong mind, a stable mind. But how did you end up in your bed? Unless…

Then, POOF!
The lights go out!

To Oz? To Oz!
We're off to see the Wizard! The Wonderful Wizard of OZ!
We hear he is a Wiz of a Wiz, if ever a Wiz there was.
If ever or ever a Wiz there was, the Wizard of Oz, is one because,
because, because, because, because, because,
because of the wonderful things he does!
We're off to see the Wizard! The Wonderful Wizard of

Oz!

An interesting and intense conference debate is in session. Let us pretend we are flies on the wall.

Imagination: "But it was I who first touched So-and-So! Therefore, I feel as though I, Imagination, should be the one to transport So-and-So back home. And the good news is that what I, Imagination, have to give, is indeed more exceptional than mere good news. Besides, the first touch is always the greatest touch!"

Faith: "Big brother? It is indeed true that you were privileged to be the first among us to touch So-and-So. However, it is truly MY touch of faith that So-and-So will need to rely on for the remainder of So-and-So's earthly existence. Remember?"

Gifted: "Now slow down, big sis. You're about to outrun yourself. Now I admit, your touch of faith truly is powerful. But? And you know I've always been proud of my but. So let me start over. But? It is MY touch that will make So-and-So's travel back home more exhilarating. Without me, So-and-So would not have half as much fun on this trip. No offense, my big brothers and sisters, but neither one of you are half as much fun as I am to hang-out with. Because everything I deliver…is special."

Character: "There! You see, baby sister? There is the problem – fun! None of us should desire that So-and-So have more fun than So-and-So can possibly handle. That is not in So-and-So's best interest. And Gifted? You are more than a handful, young lady. And every single one of us knows that if we allow So-and-So to become distracted by the promotions and the prosperity of So-and-So's gifts, then So-and-So's gifts will most definitely get out-of-hand, and will eventually lead So-and-So down the wrong path. And it is all of our duty and responsibility to make sure that So-and-So stays on that straight and narrow path. And neither one of you can deny the fact that it is MY touch of character that helps one magnanimously to stay on the right path!"

Wisdom: "Well, well. Little brother? Well said. I must say that was the most inspiring speech, and by far the most intelligent display of deliberation I have heard thus far. And coming from me, that is saying a lot. So bravo to you, my little brother. Now, big brother Imagination? Yes, your touch is certainly eye-opening. Big sister Faith? Yes, your touch is certainly life-changing. Baby sister Gifted? Yes, your touch is certainly quickening. And now back to you, my little brother. Yes, your touch of character is most certainly critical and extremely crucial! But each of you will have to agree, it is MY touch of wisdom that will enable So-and-So to accept the things So-and-So cannot change, courage to change the things So-and-So can, and wisdom to know the difference. Now, each of you meditate on that."

Courage: "Grunt. Grunt. Grrrrrr. Grunt."

Humility: "Hmmm? Ahhhh. Ohhhh. Yeaaaah!"

Grace: "Little brother Courage? Baby brother Humility? You know how much I adore both of you guys. And I honestly do respect your honest opinions. However, after all of these years I honestly still cannot comprehend a single word from either one of you two dodo birds! So then, let me just say this to all the rest of you. All of your touches are amazingly incredible. But MY touch of Grace is incredibly Amazing! Enough said."

Queen Mother Purpose: "Silence. Listen, my children. And this goes for all of you, including you, Courage and Humility. There is no need for you to carry on about whose touch is more significant than all the others. Every last one of you are equally important to So-and-So. And every last one of you are also equally important to each other. Your Mother is so very proud of each of you for how skillfully you all successfully executed your individual job assignments. So, my beautiful children, my charming sons and my lovely daughters, now you all know how your Mother feels about unity. So then, all together now, be good little boys and girls and tell your dear Mother whose touch it was that allowed each of us to be a valuable part of So-

and-So's invaluable life?"

All, except for Courage and Humility: "Yours, Mother dear! PURPOSE!"

Queen Mother Purpose: "Now that's what's up."

The spooky darkness and silence returns without a warning. From out of the morbid climate of gloom and doom, a man's unrecognized voice speaks.

"Let there be light."

Instantaneously, the "light switch" is flipped back on, and everything is bright again. You are standing in the dead center of a beach island. No, not quite. A paradise island? Yes...no. A fantasy island. Yes, like that old popular television show of the late '70s. It's a fantasy island, a cinematic scenery to behold!

The island is not huge. It is alive with beautiful palm trees, mango trees, and coconut trees. It is alive with scattered oasis,' enchanting lagoons with waterfalls, pink flamingos, peacocks, and doves, exotic colorful plants and lovely lush emerald-green grass, and an astonishing rainbow that stretches from the East shore to the West shore. And what is most intriguing about this fantasy island, which is unlikely to be on any of the world's governments' radar, is the fact that it is totally surrounded by cotton white fluffy clouds instead of the ocean.

You have yet to release the royal golden scepter; you're holding onto it as if your life depended on it. All of a sudden, POOF! You are now completely surrounded by nine people, seated on solid gold thrones, all dressed in long white robes. You're startled at first, but then a sigh of relief escapes your lungs. You smile, because nine familiar faces are smiling at you.

Big brother Imagination, as jolly as ever, gives you a "thumbs-up" signal. He pokes his stomach with that same thumb. And then he shows off his scary choppers.

Big sister Faith smiles at you and giggles. Then she gently caresses her right cheek.

Baby sis Gifted playfully blows you a kiss, touches her

left cheek, and winks her eye at you. Then, she kicks up her feet from underneath her robe. And guess what? She is wearing your missing pair of thick red comfy thermal socks! She sticks out her tongue at you, and then laughs.

Big brother Character grins and nods at you. Then he rests his left hand on his right shoulder, and pats it twice.

Big sister Wisdom smirks at you. The she adjusts her hideous, ancient, senior citizen bifocals.

Little brother Courage salutes you like a soldier. Then, with that same hand he pounds the left side of his chest once with his fist.

Baby brother Humility glances down at the time on his platinum and diamond Rolex, then points two fingers at his cool mirrored-lens shades. Then he points those same two fingers at you. And then, with his index finger, he touches the top of his chest, right above his heart.

Big sister Grace smiles and waves her right hand at you. Then, she balls her fist with that same hand and flexes her bicep muscle.

And last but definitely not least, Queen Mother Purpose…wait. Her cellphone is ringing. She answers it, but tells the caller that she will call them back. Hillary Clinton was on the other line. Anyway, she holds up the "peace-sign" at you. Then she kisses her two fingers, and touches her forehead with them, which is covered by her all white Queen Nefertiti crown.

Nine familiar smiling faces. Well, eight smiling faces. Nine new friends for life. And so, your spirit is lifted. And rightfully so. Yet, in your gut you have the strongest feeling that a tenth Traveler is missing. Could it just be your imagination? Or could you be supernaturally receiving an unction due to being "pregnant with purpose"? Well? I have a gut-feeling that your gut-feeling is about to be satisfied.

While you are pondering on these thoughts, that unrecognized man's vigorous voice speaks again. The speaker Himself however, is nowhere to be found. Yet, His presence is felt everywhere around you! And His voice? His voice…is of Another World!

"So-and-So…"

Spooked, you look up! The Darth Vader-like voice is coming from above. All nine Travelers spring up simultaneously from their royal golden thrones, and stand at attention like a military platoon.

"…Congratulations."

You kneel down on one knee, lay down the scepter, and bow your head in humble reverence to this Sovereign Voice.

"You have successfully passed my test. Instead of getting angry at me and cursing My Holy Name once you made the connection that you and the dying patient in ICU were the same person, like most of My human creations would do, you shed tears of surrender to My will. And the only way anyone is humanly capable of surrendering to My will, is by either purposely or unintentionally combining their Imagination, their Faith, their Gift, their Character, their Wisdom, their Courage, their Humility, their Grace, and their Purpose, to produce the most powerful thing I have ever created…Unconditional Love."

At this point, tears are uncontrollably streaming from the corners of your eyes. Once again, your 20/20 vision is diminished.

"Furthermore, So-and-So, you have successfully traveled beyond the limits of time and into the future, through My creation of Nothingness, which is the endless journey of My creation of Eternity. Unlike most of My human creations, you possessed the willpower and the determination and the fortitude to walk by faith and not by sight through the absolute darkest darkness, which is My creation of the Abyss, which mortal men refer to as black holes in outer space. So-and-So, you have traveled the furthest distance that a human being can travel and still survive. And it was your Unconditional Love that enabled you reach your unknown destination…your *Final Destination*."

You are not the only person on this paradise of an island shedding tears, now. As you look around, your soul is overtaken by gratitude. All nine Travelers are standing, smiling, and crying tears of joy…especially big brother Imagination. Crying like an infant who needs his smelly diaper changed. But please don't tell him I said that! Okay? Thanks!

"As soon as your teardrops of Unconditional Love dripped upon the face of your dying body in that hospital room, you immediately changed the trajectory of your destiny. So-and-So, your Unconditional Love changed the course of your future. And so, my answer to your last question, is yes. You are dying of stage four stomach cancer. That is why My angel, Imagination, chose to touch you on your belly. He imagined that you were healed…"

Blind-sided, you spin and look at big brother Imagination, with your jaw dropped. He is looking at you, smiling. And yes. He is actually smiling. You are in a temporary state of shock! With disbelief, you rationalize in your head the words you have just heard. "Imagination? An angel? Really? Wow. I didn't see that coming." Imagination, an angel disguised as, well, "Imagination," nods at you while rubbing his stomach. You smile and nod back at your friend.

"Let brotherly love continue. Be not forgetful to entertain strangers: for thereby some have entertained angels unawares" (Hebrews 13:1-2, KJV).

"…And you have exactly five months, twenty-eight days, twenty-two hours, thirty-three minutes, and ten seconds of life to live. But, the good news is that I AM THAT I AM…Unconditional Love!"

All nine Travelers begin to applaud you for your triumphant victory! Now your tears are pouring down like a hard rain. The nine Travelers gradually cease giving honor unto you for your honorable accomplishment, and return to their state of calm, quiet reverence for The Sovereign Voice.

"So-and-So, I can read your mind. You are wondering if I am the tenth Traveler. Well, I am Omnipresent. Traveling does not apply to me, simply because I exist everywhere, in all places, at the same time. So-and-So, you have traveled the distance of Eternity to arrive here at this destination, and you have touched each of us in our heart, with your demonstration of Unconditional Love. Therefore, So-and-So, the tenth Traveler…is YOU!"

The nine Travelers celebrate you once again with their applause.

"Rise to your feet, So-and-So."

You obey without hesitation and, as if you were an unsuspecting fan sitting out in the audience at a David Copperfield magic show in Las Vegas, POOF! You too are now wearing a long white robe! Just like the nine angelic Travelers. You take a few seconds to check out your new gear, then you quickly return your attention upward to The Most High voice in the sky. At this point of this amazing adventure, there is not too much that can amaze you much more.

"You are the tenth Traveler. The touch of your tears has earned you a new name amongst the Hosts of Heaven. From now on, your fellow Travelers, including all whose lives you supernaturally touch, will all refer to you as Unconditional Love because you willingly surrendered to My will. To put it plainly, what your act spoke to me was; Nevertheless, my Heavenly Father, not my will, but Thine will be done."

You wipe your tears, dry your face, then crack a smile.

"So again, congratulations So-and-So. I am proud of you. Now, go and change the world. Show us what you can do with your Unconditional Love. I showed you mine when I shed my blood of Unconditional Love for you when I was crucified on that old rugged cross. Yes, I surrendered my life and died for you. And then three days later, I arose from the dead…for you."

Before you can tell The Great and Powerful Voice – whose voice resembles the undeniably recognizable voice of James Earl Jones – "Thank You," POOF! And this is the last "POOF!" I promise.

A few seconds later, your eyes open. You are awake from your slumber. You have just experienced what I call a "psyche cyclone" – a dream within a dream within a dream. So, welcome back…to Kansas. It's morning. Thirty minutes ago, there was an angry storm, but today the sun is shining magnificently.

EPILOGUE

You sit up. You yawn. You stretch out your arms. It is a new day. You are a new person. As you sit on the edge of your bed "cheesing," it dawns on you that you have just awakened from a wonderful life-changing dream within a dream within a dream! In other words--my words--a Psyche Cyclone.

The Traveler's Touch. "Traveler's" is singular, not plural. Not plural as in nine different Travelers, but singular as in one individual Traveler...YOU! Absolutely, "So-and-So." At the end of the day, this book – *The Traveler's Touch* – is all about you and YOUR touch. You are the greatest "traveler" out of the nine. And your "touch," the touch of your teardrops of Unconditional Love, *is the most powerful touch of all!*

Mathematically, it takes the collective efforts of all nine Travelers' combined touches – Imagination, Faith, Gifted, Character, Wisdom, Courage, Humility, Grace, and Queen Mother Purpose – to produce "The Godly Touch of Unconditional Love." Now that, my friend, ought to really put a smile on your face! I'm smiling too.

I know that you are familiar with The Wonderful Wizard of Oz, but have you ever heard of "The Vigorous Voice of Zo"? Say it ain't so? Well, my friend, today is your lucky day! Sit back, relax and listen, while I tell you all about the Land of Zo. It is definitely Another World! On second thought, it seems as though we have run out of time. So, my friend, do yourself a favor, and "by any means necessary" – like Brother Minister Malcom X said – make sure that you cop yourself a copy of Part 2.

Now, it is time for you to hop up off of that waterbed, go to school or go to work and...hold up! Wait a minute. What is that on the floor? You pick it up. You examine it. It appears to be a solid gold scepter! Wow! I wonder where that came from? Suddenly, you burst out laughing. You have just remembered to whom this royal golden scepter that you are holding belongs. Do you have any idea what you are going to do with it?

Personally, I would...hold up! Listen. Hear that? Sounds like more footsteps. Ahhhh yeah. Perhaps this really does mean that a sequel is on the way; COMING SOON TO A BOOKSTORE NEAR YOU! So then, until we meet again, So-and-So, happy travels...in Jesus' name!

Back to ICU...

An index finger wiggles.

Betcha didn't see that coming. Did ya?

The End

To be continued...

NOTES

Acknowledgments
1. Eleanor Roosevelt, BrainyQuote,
   http://www.brainyquote.com/quotes/quotes/e/e
   leanorroo385439.html

Chapter 1
1. Vivian Greene, *Goodreads Quotes,*
   http://www.goodreads.com/quotes/132836-life-
   isn-t-about-waiting-for-the-storm-to-pass-it-s-
   about

Chapter 4
1. Stan Lee, *Spider-Man Comic,*
   http://www.quotes.net//quote/41082
2. *Merriam-Webster,* "fun," retrieved July 22, 2016,
   http://www.merriam-
   webster.com/dictionary/fun

Chapter 6
1. *Wikipedia,* Los Angeles Angels of Anaheim,
   https://en.wikipedia.org/wiki/Los_Angeles_Ang
   els_of_Anaheim
2. *Wikipedia,* 2002 NBA Finals,
   https://en.wikipedia.org/wiki/2002_NBA_Finals
3. *Spotrac,* C.J. Wilson,
   http://www.spotrac.com/mlb/los-angeles-angels-
   of-anaheim/c.j.-wilson/
4. *Wikipedia,* C. J. Wilson,
   https://en.wikipedia.org/wiki/C._J._Wilson

5. Phil Berger, "Leonard and Duran in Rematch in November," *nytimes.com*, July 27 1989 http://www.nytimes.com/1989/07/27/sports/leonard-and-duran-in-rematch-in-november.html

6. Richard M. Nixon, *BrainyQuote*, http://www.brainyquote.com/quotes/quotes/r/richardmn402997.html

7. Afrika Bambaataa, *BrainyQuote*, http://www.brainyquote.com/quotes/quotes/a/afrikabamb556302.html

8. Nelson Mandela, *BrainyQuote*, http://www.brainyquote.com/quotes/quotes/n/nelsonmand178789.html

9. Max Lucado, *Goodreads Quotes*, https://www.goodreads.com/work/quotes/22290416-facing-your-giants-god-still-does-the-impossible

Chapter 7

1. *MetroLyrics*, Amazing Grace, http://www.metrolyrics.com/amazing-grace-lyrics-gospel.html

2. Martin Luther King, Jr. *"I Have a Dream,"* http://www.americanrhetoric.com/speeches/mlkihaveadream.htm

3. Joel Landau, "Lithuania strongman lifts world record 1,155 pounds," *nydailynews.com*, March 31, 2014, http://www.nydailynews.com/news/national/lithuanian-strongman-lifts-record-1-155-lbs-article-1.1740503

4. Guinness World Records, "Fastest run 100 metres (male)," http://www.guinnessworldrecords.com/world-records/fastest-run-100-metres-(male)

Chapter 9

1. *Merriam-Webster,* "calling," Retrieved July 22, 2016, http://www.merriam-webster.com/dictionary/calling
2. *Merriam-Webster,* "destiny," Retrieved July 22, 2016, http://www.merriam-webster.com/dictionary/destiny

ABOUT THE AUTHOR

Jarrod Denard Dixon, Sr. is first and foremost a devoted and dedicated family man. He and his beautiful, anointed wife Cynthia, of twenty-six years, have two brilliant sons; Jiwann and Jarrod II. Mr. & Mrs. Dixon are also blessed with an amazing, lovely daughter-in-law; Shadé, who is married to Jiwann.

Jarrod D. Dixon is an Associate Minister at First Waughtown Baptist Church, Incorporated, which is located in his native hometown of Winston-Salem, North Carolina. He is proud to serve, for twenty-six years, under the leadership of his dynamic Pastor, Rev. Dennis W. Bishop.

Minister Dixon has been preaching the Gospel of Jesus Christ for sixteen years, since 2000. His primary Kingdom Assignment is men's ministry, of which via the Anointing of the Holy Spirit he passionately and radically exhorts men, Christian and non-Christians, to "come up higher!"

In July of 2015, Minister Dixon received his accredited Associates Degree in Ministry with a Concentration in Christian Counseling/Christian Psychology from Vintage Bible College and Seminary, located in Winston-Salem, NC. Thus, he is currently active as a Certified Christian Counselor in his city, where he is busy counseling at least twice a week – fulfilling his God-given calling to heal damaged relationships, unhealthy marriages, broken families, and emotionally hurting and psychologically perplexed individuals through his Spiritual Gifts of "a word of wisdom" and "a word of knowledge."

Jarrod is also divinely endowed with the artistic gifts of drawing and creative writing. He is an aspiring Screenwriter (associated with the Writer's Guild of America East), a Nationally Published Poet (Poetry.com "COME UP HITHER" – his Inspirational Poetry Collection Chapbook, and Guest Poet featured in the Anthology – "Where the Mind Dwells"), and an Author ("The Traveler's Touch"). His inspirational writings, aside from sermons, whether Poetry Collections or Book Projects, are "ministry tools" that Minister Dixon uses to build up the Kingdom of God and help change lives.

Jarrod D. Dixon, Minister/Counselor/Writer, has rooted his entire ministry in the Biblical Foundation of his favorite Scripture, which is Philippians 1:6.

"Being confident in this very thing, that He which hath begun a good work in you will perform it until the day of Jesus Christ." (KJV)